AF240884

Down Syndrome,
So What!

Éléonore Laloux

Down Syndrome, So What!

In collaboration with Yann Barte

Max Milo
TÉMOIGNAGE

Max Milo Éditions, Paris, 2023
www.maxmilo.com
ISBN : 978-2-315-01228-2

1. I'm not Poison

I know, sometimes I make gestures that can be disturbing, like talking to myself, making mimicry... But we're not poison! We're like other people and we live like other people. I'm making an effort and talking to myself less and less. I've got an extra chromosome, that's all. My father says it's the "happiness chromosome": I have trisomy 21.

Jean-Didier Vincent, a geneticist, called us "poison" on France Inter. It hurts me and makes me angry. My father has the radio on full blast at home and I listen downstairs. It's the program La tête au carré, October 5, 2012. My mother gets angry: "This is unacceptable!"

I wish doctors would stop saying harsh words. Words that hurt and frighten. It's an insult to people with Down's syndrome and their families. On the radio, they talk about the new blood tests for trisomy 21 in early pregnancy. These tests have already been in use for a year in the United States and some European countries. "Why do we need to keep people with Down's Syndrome in the family?" Yes, that's what this biologist doctor says. He talks about people with Down's syndrome being harmful because they prevent families from being happy. I know it's just the opposite.

My father thinks like me. He says it's prejudice and ignorance. This doctor knows about the human brain, but he knows nothing about people with Down's syndrome. Not like my parents and me. Not personally.

I tell my father we have to file a complaint. Actually, it's my turn to complain. He has no right to treat us like this. We can be happy and give happiness. My parents write him a letter. I'm posting a video on Dailymotion to tell him what I think of his words. He hasn't replied. He hasn't apologized. He didn't say anything.

I don't accept these labels: "handicapped", "chromosomal aberration". That's what my parents were told when I was born: I'm a "chromosomal aberration". So, of course, it's scary! But it's not a handicap. It's a treatable disease, and researchers need to create "treatment platelets[1]". My parents think it's a handicap to be a bit slow, but I reject that word. I'd like to reassure

---

1. Here, Éléonore is talking about the possibility of finding a drug treatment in the form of tablet blister packs. We have deliberately retained her expression. (NdE)

mothers. We mustn't shock them like that. They need to talk about it. It's a genetic disease that's not hard to bear, but you have to live with it. We need to help research and, above all, provide information and reassurance. But we must also respect the parents' choice. If they don't want to keep the child, that's fine. But it's still a shame.

2. All Blue

I call my parents "the lovers": "Bonjour les amoureux![2]", "Ça va les amoureux?[3]" Actually, their names are Manu and Maryse. They're always happy to see me. They give me lots of love and good cheer. And I give them a helping hand when they're not doing well. People like being with me because I'm always smiling. And they all make me happy: my parents, my brother, my family, my colleagues...

I fight to live. Ever since I was born. And I'm glad I'm here, otherwise I'd never have been able to play electric guitar, cook, go to concerts or meet up with my dad on the Mac, thanks to FaceTime, to chat with the webcam. I love it all. And when sometimes I'm not feeling well,

---

2. "Hello, lovers!"
3. "How are you, lovers?"

I put on some music and write. That's how I clear my head and feel much better.

I was born in Arras on August 26, 1985. I weigh two kilos six. A few hours later, I was transferred to the neonatal pathology center at the local hospital: I was cyanotic. This is where my older brother Mathurin had been treated, three years earlier. He was born prematurely, at seven months and two days. This is also where my other brother, Valentin, was born the following year. He died an hour after his birth. We don't know why, perhaps because of a drug given to my mother to delay childbirth.

So, for me, my mother was a little scared. She took every precaution, right from the start. She changed obstetricians and maternity hospitals. She had ultrasounds, agreed to a cerclage to keep me in the womb, and rested at home for five months with a caregiver.

At the maternity hospital, three days after my birth, the doctors decided to give my mother pills to stop her milk coming in, without asking her opinion. They said she shouldn't get attached to me. The obstetrician pulls my father aside in the corridor to tell him that I have a heart defect and am a "chromosomal aberration". What a word! I might die in a fortnight or three weeks, we don't really know. Besides, I'm blue.

My father has already printed the birth announcements. So he hastily adds a note about my health. It's still stuck in my photo album: "Éléonore's state of health is very critical. May your thoughts or prayers help her to stay with us." The prayers are for their family. They're all believers. My parents don't give a damn about God, especially my mother. She can't look after him.

When we explain everything to them, my parents are confused and shocked. What's more, they know nothing about Down's Syndrome. They trust doctors, but think it's crazy to ask them not to get attached to me.

My mother doesn't get much support, except from the medical staff and her family. She hardly ever visits the maternity ward. People are very uncomfortable because of my Down's syndrome. She doesn't have many presents for me. But with Valentin, it was worse... One of my mother's friends tells her I'm a "heavy handicap". And as she has worked with people with Down's syndrome, my parents are even more afraid.

People ask my mother, "But why didn't you know you were carrying a Down's syndrome child? Hadn't you had an amniocentesis?"

My mother didn't know, no. Besides, she wouldn't have had an amniocentesis because she was young. She was 29. I know she's glad she didn't know. She says she might have made "the biggest mistake of her life". Out of fear, because she didn't know anything and because she didn't know me yet. My father, too, is happy that I was born.

At the Neonatal Pathology Center, the doctors have other, gentler words. Because over there, people know all about babies' problems. It was even a doctor who put my parents in touch with AISET, a departmental association for parents of Down's syndrome children, which my father would head a few months later. Thanks to Dr Théret, my parents met the Tô family, while I was still at the Neonatal Pathology Centre.

The Tôs have a daughter, Fleur, with Down's Syndrome. When my parents arrive home, Fleur is playing the piano. She's 12 years old. They're a happy family, just like any other. That's what reassures my parents: to see a happy family like any other with a Down's syndrome child. Besides, my mother thinks it's maybe not her fault that she's had complicated pregnancies, that it can happen to anyone, even doctors like Fleur's parents. The father is an obstetrician and the mother an industrial doctor.

My parents aren't allowed to hug me, or even touch me. I spend most of my time sleeping. That's the way it used to be. Even the doctors didn't know that a sick baby's contact with its parents was important. Only the nurses were allowed to touch me and wash me.

In mid-September, my mother is finally able to hug me. I have the photo in my album, and I think it's really beautiful.

On November 4, after two and a half months in intensive care, I was discharged with my health still in good shape. My parents remember the date. They still tell me the story very often. I'm skinny and I can't breathe very well. My condition isn't reassuring, and neither are the doctors. Some are very pessimistic, but others give my parents hope.

I was baptized twenty days later by the priest who had married my parents. They baptized me because they were completely lost, and it was easier to get my paternal grandparents, who were very Catholic, to accept me.

It happens in the living room, on the sofa I think, with just my parents, my brother Mathurin, my grandparents, my godfather and my godmother. I'm still in poor health. I breathe badly every night and my parents get up all the time to position me properly. Because of my heart defect. I get out of breath with every bottle. So I'm fed in bits and pieces. At 4 months, I still have seven meals. I also have an oxygen tank next to my crib, which we take with us wherever we go, to the hospital or to my grandparents'.

I have to be hospitalized often because of my respiratory discomfort and because of infections. Almost every month. I don't gain weight. I get tired just drinking my bottle, so I don't have time to push. My mother told me that it takes me half an hour to drink thirty milliliters. But that's not why I'm short today. I'm one metre forty-one. People with Down's syndrome are short, that's just the way it is.

Apart from my health problems, I'm said to be an easy child. Fortunately for my poor parents, because I have quite a few health problems...

3. A Fine Mess

"It was a piece of shit!" That's what Professor Binet said to my parents as they left the operating room.

At 1 year old, I only weigh five kilos seven and I still have a lot of health problems. My parents are exhausted. They get up more than ten times a night, each in turn, to sit me up when I choke.

My heart failure is threatening to damage my lungs. I need surgery. It's a long and very dangerous operation. But we have no choice. I went to the hospital in Lille, which sent me to the Marie Lannelongue Surgical Center in Plessis-Robinson. It was there that I underwent open-heart surgery on September 9, 1986 by Professor Binet. The operation lasted twelve hours.

It takes seven times my volume of blood for this operation. So, to support me, teachers and parents donate blood at the Louez Dieu secondary school, where my father is an art teacher. The blood donation van sets up in the courtyard, and all day long, people come and go. There were over a hundred of them. There was even an article in *La Voix du Nord*. My father knows the school principal, Henri Vignolle, well. Today, he's retired and takes care of undocumented migrants in Calais. He brings them food in his truck, washes their clothes and gives them showers.

The aftermath of my operation was even more complicated. The next day, the doctors had to reopen me because a catheter was stuck in a suture. Three weeks later, I developed a staphylococcus aureus infection. I'm not sure what that is - it's another word I need to write down in my notebook. But I do know that it, too, is "one hell of a bugger". That's what my father says. Then came a third operation for mediastinitis. As a result, I have a very large scar on my sternum. They say it's "not a pretty sight".

I'm staying in intensive care until the end of October. I'm still in a sterile environment and my parents can't see me. The surgeons tell them that if I were an adult, I'd let myself die because I'm in so much pain. They also warn them that I only have a 50-50 chance of getting out of this, and that they may decide not to continue with me.

I still have to fight to show that I want to live. But I can't speak. In any case, my vocal cords are stuck because of the tubes I have in my mouth to be fed.

And then my parents get to see me, finally. They look at me through a glass window. My arms and feet are tied. I'm crucified, with my head stuck and pipes everywhere. They speak and I hear them. I smile as I recognize their voices. They're upset. My parents are always moved when they tell me this story.

For three and a half months I struggle and smile at my parents to reassure them. I eat a diet with lots of protein to encourage tissue regrowth and the closing of my sternum. I have lots of bandages and tubes all over my mouth and nose... even when I come out of intensive care. My mother takes some off for photos, so that people can see something of my head. But I stick my tongue out in all the shots because I don't have time to see the speech therapist at the hospital to do my exercises.

On November 23, all my pipes are removed. I came home a few days before Christmas. My brother Mathurin was very worried the whole time I was in hospital. He's 4 and a half. When I came home, he said to me: "I'm glad you didn't die.

4. Come on, Let's Go!

"Go for it!" That's how my parents always boosted me, right from birth. And it helps me. Even today, when I go shopping at Leclerc, they hurry me along. We go our separate ways and I try to finish before they do. I use the purchase scan, go to the checkout, pay and wait on a bench for them to finish their shopping. My father goes quietly with me. My mother's a bit fast, but that's fine too.

Ever since my parents met the Tô family when I was born and saw how happy Fleur looked, they've been hopeful and have decided to help me as much as they can to make sure I keep progressing. They constantly stimulate me. They do everything they can to help me become independent as quickly as possible. They're happy every time I do something new, no matter how simple. They watch for the slightest progress: the first time I sit up, the first time I take the bottle cap in my hand... And they photograph everything.

My parents also took me to see all the specialists. They noticed that I stuck out my tongue as a baby, so they took me to the speech therapist first. This is often the case with Down's syndrome babies: their tongues fall out. Every week, we go to Douai to see a speech therapist who knows babies with Down's Syndrome very well. We go there with my oxygen tank in the car. The speech therapist shows my parents how to stimulate my tongue, how to make my lips firmer, by feeding me with a teaspoon, pressing it against my tongue. I quickly gave up bottles and switched to baby food. My parents even stuck the labels of the Guigoz jars with apricots, apples or carrots in my photo album.

My parents consulted everywhere: a physiotherapist to straighten my feet and do breathing exercises, and a psychomotricist. Then podiatrists for my flat feet, an orthodontist and an orthoptist to correct my squint. I have to wear a cover over my glasses for almost two years because I squint too, and I have finger exercises where I have to squint even more to correct. I look at my finger or at an approaching pen and I have to keep my eyes on it until it's almost on my nose. My parents also take me to pediatricians, psychologists, cardiologists, pneumologists, stomatologists... They run around, taking me to specialized consultations in Paris, to the

Jérôme Lejeune Institute and then to Necker Hospital. Some doctors don't try too hard to understand the causes and say that my health problems are due to my trisomy. But that's a bit easy... So my parents continue to seek advice elsewhere.

5. War Declared

I don't like being around children. I'm afraid of their games, their cries, their sudden movements. I can't keep up, it's too fast for me. And when they fight, I'm terrified.

When I was 3, I started kindergarten. It was a new ordeal for me. My parents are a bit afraid that I won't fit in, that I'll be pushed around. I'm three apples high. I'm very small for my age.

My parents are very proud to see me off with my little schoolbag on my back, like my big brother Mathurin. He's at another school, still in the public sector. My parents absolutely want me to go to a mainstream school, but they can't keep me in the public sector. So I went to the Sainte-Marie-de-la-Présentation school in Arras. I started school for the first time in 1988. No problems, no tears. I'm pretty cool and adapt easily.

In the beginning, I often stand back in the playground. I don't like the hustle and bustle. Noises scare me, like ambulance or fire sirens. It reminds me of all my hospitalizations. Even today, when I hear sirens, I cover my ears. My mother always tells me: "Go on, Eleonore, don't be afraid", so that I'll go towards the others, or just walk into a store… Sometimes she even pushes me really hard in the back so that I move forward. I take a step and she pushes me again. And that helps. Even to start a drawing or an exercise, I need someone to push me. I'm afraid of failing.

Then I started to reach out to other children, to have friends. That reassured my parents. But I'm still a bit of a recluse. My brother says I had "a parallel world". I talked to imaginary beings, I was in my own bubble. Several times, my parents lost me at Monoprix. Because I leave, I wander around on my own, following the aisles and forgetting all about my family. That's how I got my first spanking. My parents were in a panic.

At Hardelot beach on the Côte d'Opale, they were really scared too. I was 2 or 3 years old. That's when they decided to buy me a pretty little gold-plated bracelet. They had it engraved with my first name and their telephone number. So I'd never get lost again. I still wear it today. I have a small wrist.

So when my brother and I go scouting, my mother has to explain that I have to be careful. If I meet a donkey, I can stay and chat with him and completely forget that the group is moving on. It's true that I like donkeys. They're gentle, but you have to give them grass and carrots to make them walk. At the À Petits Pas association in Ruisseauville, I do a lot of hiking with donkeys.

In kindergarten, things always went well. And we didn't talk about being behind in school yet. I did all my schooling in an open environment. It was very complicated for my parents.

Every year, the guidance committees want to send me to special schools. And every year, my parents go to war with the school and have to fight to keep me there. They have to explain, argue, convince. I often see them despair and cry. Even my father.

At home, we have mountains of files for the CDES (commission départementale de l'éducation spéciale), year after year, with educational projects, reports from speech therapists, psychologists, test reports, letters to "Monsieur l'inspecteur d'Académie..." It's thanks to my parents that I grow up with children like any other, that I make progress and gain self-confidence. But they often have to move me to another school. Every time they don't want me anymore, they move me. My parents aren't too keen on the presentation teacher in the middle section of kindergarten. They don't think I'll get on well with her, so they send me to Saint-Joseph.

5. War Declared

The 1990s were exhausting for my parents. Every year, they have to prove my skills and progress. I do test collections. Tests that are often unsuitable for people like me with Down's syndrome. Tests that don't mean much, according to my parents and Dr. Leroux at Necker Hospital: the PEP test, the Terman-Merrill test… We don't really know what they measure.

My parents also collect reports. Report from teacher X and headmistress Y, report from the physiotherapist, report from the speech therapist, report from the pediatrician Bernard Théret who has been following me for years.

And always, at the end of the letter, the same decision from the commission "proposing that your child be sent to a specialized establishment at the start of the next school year". Every year, my parents choke when they read the letter: "The elements and the good of the child justify his admission to a specialized establishment."

So my parents, crestfallen and disgusted, went to war again. They wrote a letter of appeal to the CDES, and asked three teachers and a nursery assistant to support their request to remain in the nursery class. A new report from the speech therapist, then from the physiotherapist, a new report from the teacher Mrs X and the headmistress Mrs Y, a request for an informal appeal, then a request for a contentious appeal.

The school inspectorate doesn't care; they don't think I belong in a mainstream school. So my parents rallied the whole school around me. They got over a thousand parents to sign in support of me. But that wasn't enough. So they hired a lawyer, Maître Vincent Potié. "Your daughter will never be Mozart or Einstein". You're going to kill her by trying to get her to study. Vincent Potié remembers this phrase from the president of the commission, hurled at my parents. But he knows that school, like an open-plan business, encourages my personal development and independence. Every year, my parents find themselves in court. They're called "irresponsible". I don't like that. But they still refuse to send me to a special school. They always do.

Finally, I entered a mixed class. Kindergarten in the morning until ten o'clock, then preparatory classes until four-thirty. I'm still in the mainstream and at Saint-Joseph. I'm just slower than the others. My parents have gained another year. They still support me.

My brother Mathurin is always by my side too. He protects me and encourages me. In my end-of-year nursery school show photos, you can see me at the age of 5, on the stage, crying or with a dirty grimace. In the corner of the photo, at the edge of the stage, you always see a little boy: it's Mathurin, always there to reassure me.

6. My Big Brother

Mathurin is my big brother. He's three years older than me. At 8 or 10, he's blond with beautiful eyes and a face as round as a balloon. Mat is hyperactive and a bit crazy. He's always doing something. He gets his kicks rollerblading, hurting himself all the time, but he doesn't care. He runs everywhere. Just the opposite of me. I'm a bit slow and he makes me dizzy. My parents don't know what to do with him any more, so they take him to the children's hospital because he's really too fast.

Mat and I were brought up the same way. But my parents spend a lot more time with me. With my Down's syndrome, there are a few more complications... As kids, we sleep in the same room, on bunk beds. Mat upstairs, me downstairs.

My brother is always there for me. When I'm in tears, when I'm scared, he consoles me, reassures me. He tells me to keep going. He encourages me and shows me the way, and I trust him. When I have a problem in judo or skiing, climbing on a merry-go-round or getting into a place, when I have moments of shyness in a crowd or at a family meal, he looks after me, pushes me to go.

He also calms me down. When he takes me to the physiotherapist, I sometimes panic on the main boulevard in Arras because of an ambulance or fire siren. I get completely stuck at the end of the crosswalk, my feet nailed to the ground. Mat tells me it'll pass, that it won't do anything to me. He takes me by the hand.

I'm still very close to him, but we don't have the same friends. He sometimes introduces me to his own. On birthdays, for example. Sometimes, he explains to them what I have, my Down's syndrome. He's a bit of a teacher, because his friends don't know anything about the disease.

At home, we do puzzles, coloring and Lego stuff. When we get home from school, we do our homework at the same table in the kitchen. Mat finishes in two seconds. It takes me much longer, and then I write with my nose glued to my paper. My brother and I have also shared activities since we were little, like judo and scouting.

Mathurin is teaching me to swim. We were on vacation in Corsica, at Porto-Vecchio. It's the best memory I have of my brother. I'm 5 or 6 years old and I've got corks all around my waist and arms. That's what I call the floats:

the "plugs". I'm in the sea trying to do fathoms. I pass from my father to my brother, who holds out his arms. My brother helps me. He's proud of me. And Corsica is so beautiful! It's full of black pigs. There are herds of them everywhere. On the road, everywhere. They stop us getting through. My father honks his horn, but there are always others coming along and rubbing the car. I like watching the pigs. And playing on tree trunks, balancing, while my parents and brother go parasailing.

Several times a year, I go on vacation with my brother to my paternal grandparents' in Moyenneville. Moyenneville is a small village in the countryside. It's where my father was born. My grandparents are farmers and raise animals. I'm fascinated by sheep. They have beautiful eyes like my brother.

I love touring the farm with Mat. It's huge. One by one, we visit all the buildings, the barn, the garden, the pigs, the cows, the chickens, the rabbits, the fruit storage area...

Sometimes my father holds me astride the dog while my brother drives the tractor. That's how I follow him around the fields. With my cousins, everyone fights to get on the *John Deere*. In summer, we play in the inflatable pool, I pick flowers in the garden... And sometimes, we spend vacations further afield, at the beach. My father and I bury Mathurin in the sand. Except for his head, so he can breathe a little.

In Arras, too, there's a lot of fun to be had, especially during the ducasse. It's a funfair from our part of the world. I go on the rides with the pom-poms. I'm always the one who wins the free rides. I like the rides that go up and down like a yo-yo. I also like duck fishing and bumper cars. My brother takes one car and I take another, so we can bump into each other.

My brother can't stand being spoken to differently, as if I were 2 years old. At the Artois Judo Club, even though I'm a yellow belt, he even tells the teacher to speak to me normally, to respect me. He takes the initiative. So the teacher corrects himself. Until I stop judo, when I get my green belt, he talks to me like any other student. Mat trains me. It's gentler with him. He teaches me holds and falls.

My brother and I are also Scouts. Not in the same team: I'm with the Cubs, he's a Scout, in blue. Over there, I'm just like the others. But we have to walk fast and I can't always keep up. It's a nice group and I have great buddies, like Mélanie, with whom I sleep in the tent.

I like my brother. He's nice. Plus, he's got some really funny tricks. For example, when we give him injections, it makes him laugh.

7. Good Manners

At the age of 7, I'm a pleasant, easygoing little girl. I'm still a little anxious when my parents walk into a room next door, but I'm also more likely to go up to strangers. I have some speech difficulties, but I understand everything I'm told. That's what the commission reports say.

As my parents have to show my abilities and progress every year to keep me in a mainstream environment, I continue to take batteries of tests. I'm asked to draw a picture, stand on one foot, catch a ball, touch my thumb, do puzzles, imitate gestures, sort cards into categories or repeat sentences, words, numbers... I have some memory problems, especially with numbers.

At home, my mother teaches me to read and write. She hangs words all over the walls of my room. Words in big letters: "Papa, maman, Mathurin, maison, mamie..." and pronouns "il, elle, nous, vous..." That way, I learn to read and also to articulate. She makes me repeat the words, and I like that. At 2, I recognize a few words. Around the age of 4 or 5, I start learning to read with the school life assistant and the speech therapist, who teaches me a gesture method: I have to associate a gesture with each sound. I have a book called *Bien lire et aimer lire*. I love this book.

I started writing and counting at the age of 6. I wrote my first letters to my parents when I was 10, at Cub Scout camp with my brother. I like reading today. I read all the time. I've just started reading *Les Trois Mousquetaires*, and at home I read animal magazines like *30 millions d'amis*, people magazines, *TV magazines* and *Presto!* a small regional rock magazine where my mother occasionally writes about concerts. And whenever I see a word that's a bit complicated, I write it down in a notebook with the definition from my big Robert Collège. I have five notebooks like that. I put in words like "hypothétique", "hibernation", "australe", "entremise", "élytre" or "lapidation".

My parents want me to be respected. They insist that I'm polite. They ask me to say "hello", "goodbye", "thank you", to look at the person I'm talking to when I speak - and not at my feet, but I often forget that. They also ask me to behave properly. They want me to be accepted everywhere, so ever since I was a little girl, I've had to be polite and behave myself, at the table, outside, in the street... Don't put my elbows on the table, don't talk to yourself, and that's a bit more complicated. Don't grind your teeth... I often grind my teeth when I'm tired. At night, I wear a mouthpiece to prevent them from wearing out.

Even today, my parents still make comments. They wait until we're alone and explain to me that what I've done isn't right. They tell me not to pull up my panties in public, not to grope myself while watching TV... "That's something I should only do when I'm older. I should only do that when I'm on my own." My mother laughs when I say that. She says, "No, you don't *have* to do that, but you *can* if you're on your own." I shouldn't twitch my nose either. I mustn't spread my legs too much when I'm in a skirt, but I mustn't cross them when I'm in a suit either, because that's bad for my legs. I have to be pleasant, not make a fuss, not look down when people talk to me... I've said this before, but it's true that I do it a lot. I know it helps to be told all this.

8. Stephanie's Room

When I go to Stephanie's house, I go straight up to her room. We slam the door to get some peace and quiet. We put on some music and sing and play. Stephanie is my girlfriend. When I'm with her, I feel at home. Stéph' and I are almost the same age. I'm five or six months older than her, that's all.

We've been together since I was 4.

We met at the Down Up association my father set up almost as soon as I was born. Well, it had another name before that. It's an association that supports the families of people with Down's syndrome. Because Stephanie is triso, like me.

In the bedroom, we play with Polly Pockets: little dolls in heart-shaped pink boxes. In summer, we go swinging in the garden, or tobogganing. We tell each other our secrets on the sofa, too, or heckle a bit. But not too loud. I have to be a bit careful because Stephanie is wearing a neck brace. Her cervical spine is fragile and she'll have to keep it on for quite a few more years. She's not allowed to do any violent sports.

Stephanie has a big scar like me, very long but thin. Her mother Anne-Marie explained to me what she had on the back of her neck. I was touched. Anne-Marie also has a scar, on her leg. She showed it to me. That's why she prefers to wear pants. In the car, when we were talking, I put my hand on her leg to show her that I'm there with her, forever. Anne-Marie tells me I'm part of her life.

I ask Anne-Marie lots of questions and we talk a lot. Anne-Marie teaches me things. For example, she tells me how the underground miners lived and worked. She tells me secrets too. I write her little bills to tell her how much I love her, that she's my great girlfriend. I sign them "la gazelle". She loves me very much. We hug. Stephanie's parents take me everywhere, to play parks, pedal-boating at Le Fleury and even on vacation.

When Stephanie was very young, I didn't see much of her, because she often went to the United States. She had to follow a program called the Doman method. She had to crawl and walk on all fours for ten meters, stuff like that. Every six months, she had to go over there to do her exercises, so she didn't go to school anymore.

All those trips were expensive, so her parents stopped. Stephanie started kindergarten. That's how she got to Presentation like me, but not in the same class. And it's in middle school that I finally meet her again.

9. Photocopies

Mrs. Bisbrouck is always telling us, "Now you're not in elementary school, you're in collège!" And the four of us are really proud to be in collège: Steph', Alexandre, Ludivine and me. Mrs. Bisbrouck is our new teacher at the Louez Dieu middle school in Anzin-Saint-Aubin. She's the one who created our class, in a former teachers' room. The first CLIS (school integration class) in Pas-de-Calais. It was the Down Up association and the school principal who asked for it to be opened. I was 13 when I started secondary school in September 1998.

We all have Down's Syndrome, except Ludivine who has a mild intellectual disability. But we remain in a mainstream environment and share the playground, canteen, refectory, theater and choir activities with the others... and even a few English lessons.

A few days after the start of the school year, Mrs. Bisbrouck asks us: "Who can go and make photo-copies in the secretary's office?" I immediately raise my finger: "I'll do it!" But I can't get past the classroom door. I just can't. I'm paralyzed. Just like on the main boule-vard in Arras when ambulances go by with their sirens blaring She doesn't understand why. I don't know what I'm supposed to do after that door. There's a rotunda, a staircase, a hall, then you have to go into the secretariat, talk... It's too much. I can't think of all the steps.

So Mrs Bisbrouck accompanies me. She takes advan-tage of every situation to teach us things. She writes in my teaching plan: "fetch photocopies", and every time I have to do this, she accompanies me and stops a little earlier. First at the secretarial door, then in the corridor... It goes on for months. Then it's enough for me to know that she's watching me, and I'm reassured. And then one day I know how to go it alone. It also means I can go to other parts of the school on my own.

Mrs. Bisbrouck explained to me later that I had helped her in her work, without realizing it. It was this story about photocopies that gave her the idea of a "pedagogy of support" for people with Down's syndrome. I'm no longer afraid, not even of that six-metre-tall giant standing in the entrance hall. I walk past him every time I go to make photocopies. We call him Léonard. The North is the land of giants, and this one was made by students in the art class. In fact, we call him "Cré Léonard", which is what we say here for "sacred". He's got a compass in one hand and a palette of paint in the other. It's Leonardo da Vinci. He even came out during the World Cup, for the match in Lens where the French team was playing. He made his rounds at Bollaert stadium. Antoine, the school cleaner, sometimes dismantles Cré Léonard. I'm impressed when I see that.

In the classroom, I always like to participate. I also like to advise others and solve their problems. That's the way I am. Our teacher teaches us everything: history, geography, French. She teaches us all these subjects, even through drama. I especially like French and cooking. Every Thursday, we have a cooking class. The whole school smells of pizza! The other classes wonder what we do. Even the principal wants to come and have a look.

Mrs. Bisbrouck gives us a shopping list to take to the supermarket next door to buy what we need to make the pizzas. We choose the products, pay at the checkout and then cook in class. It's much more fun than math. As soon as she mentions it, Stephanie and I make funny faces. Mrs. Bisbrouck says we're "breaking down". So she reassures us: "Don't worry, girls. We're not going to do mathematics with numbers. We're going to do math with words." So we're reassured.

Stephanie and I are even closer now that we're finally in the same class. We're inseparable. I don't hesitate to tell her what I think: "I don't agree with you Stephanie", "You're a teenager and you behave like a little girl", "Steph, I don't like it when you get into mischief." When she gets into trouble, I blush as if it were me. I like things square, I'm very tidy, but Stephanie doesn't give a damn. She's hyper-bordered. I ask her if she'll do the same when she gets into her apartment and tell her that Mrs. Bisbrouck won't go to see her if it's not tidy.

Mrs. Bisbrouck doesn't mind if I talk to myself. In the classroom, she tells me I can go and talk to the walls or the windows if I feel like it. But not outside the school. She says that outside, "it has to stay in your head, not in your mouth". She explains that everyone talks to themselves, but in their heads.

She also corrects me sometimes. When I bump into the school principal, Henri Vignolle, I say, "Hi buddy!" Then Mrs. Bisbrouck says, "Good morning, Mr. Director." But he's still my buddy.

It was Henri Vignolle and my father who wanted the school to be open to students with disabilities. The idea came to them when my parents had all these problems with the school. They fought for it against the diocesan departmental management, which didn't agree. As a result, Manu became president of the school. My father is always president of something. And I like being the president's daughter. When the school opened up to the disabled, my father stepped down as president and I took over.

We also have two doctors who visit the class regularly. They work with us on the body, well-being... Once we put on relaxation music and then other music to express ourselves. I don't know why I started crying. It was so beautiful. I couldn't stop. Then they cut the music. I don't know why I was like that.

Sometimes I give talks. When I'm at Mrs. Bisbrouck's, I listen a lot to *Bitter Sweet Symphony* by The Verve and then *Pure Morning* by Placebo, so I decide to do a talk on Placebo. I prepare a questionnaire: what instrument does Brian Molko play? What's his nationality? How many members are there in the band? Where did they meet?

In January 1999, we went to see the Goya exhibition at the Musée des Beaux-Arts in Lille. It was our first outing with the class. We took the train to Arras. As soon as I got on the seat, I took out my book, as my mother had told me. When we arrived in Lille, I told Mrs. Bisbrouck: "No, we haven't arrived, it's not possible." My mother had given me "a book to read on the train", so I couldn't have arrived since I hadn't finished the book.

We had prepared our visit in class. So, we already know the paintings, but we prefer to see them in real life. Arriving at the museum, we queue for our admission

9. Photocopies

tickets. In front of us is a group of people. One of them says, staring at us, "I hope they're not coming with us!" I say to Mrs. Bisbrouck, loudly: "Madame, there's one looking at me from a corner, I don't like it." We find the group in the exhibition rooms. He's very embarrassed. Stéph', Alexandre and Ludivine go from one painting to another. A lady in the group, who was also watching us *from the corner* earlier, is looking for the name of one of the paintings, so I tell her, "It's called *Les Vieilles*."

I like this painting. There's a bit of sadness. Mrs. Bisbrouck always asks us to say what we feel. She leaves us completely free to express ourselves, and never takes us back. It's what you see that counts. And I see a lady looking at her daughter without saying a word, and a man working in the back at the harvest to feed his children. That's *Les Vieilles* for me.

When people look at us *from the corner*, Mrs. Bisbrouck sometimes makes reflections. Like when we went to see Galeries Lafayette in Paris at Christmas. There were two children with their father, all of whom climbed up onto the little footbridge to get a better look at the windows. When we got there, the wife said to her husband, "Come down quickly, kids, look what's happening!" She was talking about us. Mrs. Bisbrouck told them what she thought. And I supported her: "You did the right thing, we're not idiots!"

Mathurin spent a year in Australia. He is 15 years old. He's in a foster family. In fact, I've heard that he's already tired of two of them, and is now in a third. I'm not well without my brother. I'm seeing a psychiatrist, Dr. Grenier, because I'm really not well. I think Mathurin is dead. I don't think he's coming back. I don't hear from him anymore. And it's far away.

My mother says I have no sense of time, but a year is too long. She tells me what he's doing over there, that he's left rollerblading to go skateboarding and snow-boarding, but I don't see him. I love my brother very much and I miss him.

The following year, my maternal grandfather died, my grandfather Henri. I'm not there when it happens: I'm at a scout camp in Brittany. My brother Mathurin wrote it to me on a card. And it was my grandmother who told me later: "Your grandfather died in hospital in Arras."

I liked him, he was gentle and talked to me normally. In class, I can't stop crying. I'm so sad. In the end, it really gets on Mrs. Bisbrouck's nerves. I cry all the time and talk about my grandfather. Mrs. Bisbrouck points out that I cry most when she gives me work to do. So I stop.

I've got a boyfriend now, Alexandre. Mrs. Bisbrouck caught us kissing on the mouth in the kitchen corner of the classroom. We love each other. I said to her:

9. Photocopies

"Madame, don't tell my parents, okay? It's a secret between us..."

In the playground, there are some older 4th and 3rd graders who sometimes tease us. For example, they ask Alexandre to go and kiss someone, or they push us around. They're having fun. But we're not so amused. My father says that we have to "get over it" and that "we have to toughen up a bit", "learn to fight". Other people treat us too. Once, a girl called me a "trisotte". I tell Mrs. Bisbrouck. She explains that it's because I'm a girl and if I were a boy, she would have called me a "triso". I laughed. She went to talk to the girl anyway.

Some people in the school look at me really strangely or meanly. It hurts my feelings. Others call me a "whore", outright. On the school bus, when I come home at night, some students put chewing gum in my hair. It's happened twice. I was sitting right in front of them, at the back of the bus. It really hurt. I know it's because I have Down's Syndrome. It bothers the older kids to see me on the same bus as them. They don't understand what I'm doing here. When I show my mother my hair, she says, "It's a disgrace!"

The class is also going to Canterbury in England. We eat English cakes there. We drink tea. We even fill in a questionnaire with lots of questions about Canterbury's history. It's my favorite part of the trip. This game makes me feel intelligent. I say to myself, "That's my thing!"

Stephanie takes photos while walking. She never stops walking when she takes photos. Mrs. Bisbrouck advises her to stop and frame her photos. She doesn't understand this. I tell her to listen to Mrs. Bisbrouck. So Stéph' lends her camera to Mrs Bisbrouck to show her how it's done. Afterwards, we developed Stephanie's photos. They all turned out well, except for Mrs. Bisbrouck's, because she had put her finger in front of the lens. "That's what I call her sometimes." I tell her: "Madame, you're quite something!"

In March 2001, we went to Lélex, in the Jura, to stay at Mrs. et M. Vacher's country gîte. There are six of us in the class this year, plus Amandine and Élise. Over there, we go snowshoeing and eat tartiflette. We're going to Lake Geneva to see the swans. We even visit a cheese factory and play cards with Stephanie, Élise and the others. Philippe, Mrs. Bisbrouck's husband, wanted us all to play by the same rules, which is why he couldn't understand our game. We each had our own rules.

Élise was a little lost without her family. She often isolated herself and said she was going to call her parents with her pack of eucalyptus handkerchiefs. So in the evenings, to reassure her when she wasn't in the mood, I'd tell her to take her handkerchiefs and phone her parents. It calmed her down.

This year, at school, I'm singing *Tender* by Blur all the time, everywhere, in class, at recess... I love everything

9. Photocopies

about this song, Alex's double bass at the beginning, the chorus, Damon... I have it in my head all the time, for months on end.

"Tender is the night
lying by your side.
Tender is the touch
of someone that you love to much... "

When Mrs. Bisbrouck asks us to choose a piece of music to recite a poem, I choose this song from Blur's album *13*. And in the English class my mother gives to deaf and hearing-impaired young people, when I give a talk on Blur, I still sing this song with Julien accompanying me on guitar. He's deaf, but he feels the vibrations. I went to his place and he even has a drum kit. I like Graham's rendition of "*Oh my baby, oh my baby, oh why, oh my...*". And when I see Julien, he always sings me "*Come on, come on, come on, get through it...*" A friend of my mother's even gives me the sheet music I'm trying to play with Pierre Mordacque, my guitar teacher, with whom I've started taking lessons.

I stay for three years, until June 2001, in Mrs. Bisbrouck's class. I was already almost 16. So, to avoid being too far out of step with my age, I left the collège and entered the lycée.

10. High School Years

When I arrive at school, people look at me with big eyes, like "What are you doing here?" That's how they talk to me: "What are you doing here?" I let it slide. I'm pretty shy. But I've never been sexually assaulted. When I say that to my mother, she says:

"Ah well, lucky again!"

In 2001, I entered the private Lycée Baudimont Saint-Charles, in Arras, in a vocational integration class (CLIP). It was a bit complicated... At first, I was with students I didn't know and who didn't know me. So they look at me sideways, meanly. It's not like in CLIS where I had my friends who protected me. Over there, it's a bit tough at first. I'm slowly getting used to it, but I'm not very comfortable in my own skin.

In September of the following year, my mother was summoned to the school infirmary. She arrived in a panic. She's an English teacher next door at the same school. The nurse shows her a letter I've just written to Mathilde. A suicide note. Mathilde got scared, so she told the teacher, who told the nurse, who showed it to my mother. My parents don't know Mathilde, but I see her all the time at recess.

In the letter, I talk about Roch Voisine's song, my favorite: *Elle est ma tendresse*. I dedicate it to her, and then I talk about "sticking a knife in my stomach" because "I'm fed up with being like this". I think that's when Mathilde understands that there's something wrong. I write to her that I don't want to live with my scar anymore and that I want to die. I end with "*I love you*".

So my mother takes me to a corner of the infirmary to talk to me in private. She wants to understand. She was scared and angry at the same time. I'm going to say something rude, but I think I behaved a bit like a bitch. I'm sorry I wrote that letter. I know it's serious. My mother calls my father, who arrives shortly afterwards. I think he was really scared. The nurse advises me to see a psychiatrist. But I've already been seeing Mr. Grenier for two years. I'll tell him about this letter. He finds the words to reassure me. But I won't tell him about my scar. I don't want him to know. I'm a bit self-conscious.

My mother thinks I'm making up stories, that I like to create my own world with adult stories like in the TV shows I watch, *Seven at Home* or *Under the Sun*.

I think that's how she reassured the nurse. I met the actress Catherine Adams from *Sous le soleil,* who is the godmother of the Trisomie 21 association. She plays Blandine, Laure's mother, whose real name is Bénédicte Delmas. I've got autographs and photos of Tonya Kinzinger. In any case, I've never had any more suicidal thoughts.

After my high school classes, I sometimes meet Stephanie at her home. We play Scrabble junior, lotto and riddles in her room. We watch the *Harry Potter* DVD and then take turns singing along to CDs by Garou, Roch Voisine or Hélène Ségara. Sometimes, we also draw. Stephanie takes drawing lessons.

I prefer the guitar. I continue my lessons with Pierre Mordacque. Now, every Saturday, I have acoustic guitar. I work on the basics, notes, melody and chords. Pierre writes songs for me and takes out the scores he chooses on his computer. He wrote *Éléonore song for* me. We have fun coming up with titles and it makes me laugh. He called it *Elle est au Nord, Song.*

Sometimes Mathurin drops in at the weekend. It's been a year since he left home, but he still has the keys and comes whenever he wants. He's studying for a BTS in Calais. He's got a girlfriend called Maïté. He sees her at weekends too. I like it when my brother is happy. He's become calmer since he left. One day, I'll do what he did. I'm going to leave.

My father found a used car for Mat. Mat just got his driver's license. Now he can go to Maïté's in Neuville-Saint-Vaast. But over there, he smashed his car into a house. It's ruined now. He hadn't even had it three weeks. He got angry with a friend, so he slammed on the handbrake and off he went! We were in the Canaries with my parents. When we got back, we saw that he'd also smashed the marble table in the living room with his friends. They'd had a little party.

Once a week, I go to the speech therapist. She teaches me articulation in reading, masculine and feminine forms and tenses. She also tells me how to stop stuttering: I still stutter a lot. She gives me exercises to do in front of a mirror for swallowing. When I close my mouth, I have to put my tongue over my teeth and press my lips together. That way, my mouth stays shut. And I continue to see Carole, my physiotherapist.

For my first internship, in 2003, I worked in the high school secretariat for half-days. Then the headmistress sent me to La Belle Époque retirement home to mop the floor, clean the tables... It's really not my thing! Besides, I hate getting my hands dirty. So my parents asked me to take a part-time BEP secretarial course. I want to do administrative work and I'm desperate to learn computers.

The head of the school thinks it's weird. She's not too keen on me. She says to my parents: "It's hard enough for our BEPs to find internships or jobs. Don't even think about it for someone with Down's syndrome!" In the end, she agrees, telling my teacher to take me on, certain that it won't work out and that my parents will understand.

Except that it works. I even continued the following year. That's how I got into the educational integration unit at the vocational high school and, at the same time, into the 1st year of the secretarial BEP. I'm 19 years old. I have three hours a week of vocational training to learn the secretarial trades, in addition to general education in the group class with seven other Down's syndrome carriers.

I'm happy: I'm starting a computer course with teacher Lise-Marie De Reu. I like that. I'm also learning about office automation, mail and filing.

In computer class, I'm the only one with Down's Syndrome. So people look at me a bit strangely in the first class. The students are astonished. They wonder why I'm in this class. I'm a bit intimidated. I don't know anyone and it's very crowded. I'm accompanied by an AVS, a school life assistant. Her name is Nadège.

On the second day, I feel much more at ease. The other students see that I don't have any more difficulties than the others in the class. I'm quickly integrated. My AVS is very happy to learn with me, especially the Word program, because she knows nothing about computers and is completely lost. I help her a lot.

At first, I still need a little reassurance. At the end of a lesson, I come and snuggle up to the teacher. Lise-Marie De Reu says, "Eleonore, you know, I can't hug everyone." The whole class laughs. She explains that I'm not supposed to do that in a work situation, in a company. I have to be like everyone else.

On the third day, Mrs. De Reu puts me with Angelo, a student who's a bit speedy like my brother. He's the one I have to work with. Angelo became a real pal. He's so nice. He moves around a lot. I always have to tell him to sit still. I meet up with him at recess to talk. I'm happy too, because I can do things that the others can't do on Word and Excel. And I type with my ten fingers, without looking at the keyboard.

I'm very organized and focused when it comes to managing my files. And then I'm square and meticulous. Now I have a better command of computers, which I use almost every day. My class likes me. At school, when I'm absent, everyone asks where I am. And when there are outings with the BEP, there's always a student asking if I'm coming too, even for the law course.

That's how I get to the Saint-Omer assize court. I spend the whole day there with the class. It's really impressive! A man arrives with his wrists handcuffed. It's about a murdered child, I think. Lise-Marie De Reu is next to me, explaining everything. At noon, we go out to eat at McDonald's and then return to follow the hearing. I still have the class photo in front of the assize court building.

In September 2003, I was hospitalized for three days with pyelonephritis, a urinary tract infection. I think it was because I was holding back too much at school. Because we're not allowed to go to the toilet outside recess. My class hasn't forgotten me and that means a lot to me. At the hospital, I receive a card with a little note from everyone wishing me a good recovery.

My mother is with me. I'm delighted. She's a bit disgusted though: because of my pyelonephritis, she'll miss the Damon Albarn concert in London on December 22. She had bought her concert ticket and even the Eurostar ticket. It's Damon's only solo concert and she's a super-fan. She's even created a website about Blur. We went to see them in October, in Brussels.

It's not so bad, we have a good laugh at the hospital. We watch *Le Père Noël est une ordure* and then follow the Star Academy final with Michal. He loses out to Élodie Frégé, but she leaves him half the million euros she wins. And thanks to infusions and antibiotics, I heal fast. When I go back to school, my mother gives me a letter from the doctor allowing me to go to the toilet whenever I want. I don't want to go back to hospital.

This high school period with CLIP is really fun. I go on outings with my friends Stephanie, Victoria and Ségolène. We even went to Agny, a few kilometers from

Arras, with the class and my old judo teacher, Marc. With tandems donated to the school by the Rotary Club. I pedal with Astrid. We visit a mill to see how flour is made. We sleep in a gîte and have fun evenings where I make pancakes and do Turkish dances...

11. The Spider that Walks Backwards

With Pierre, my acoustic guitar teacher, we had trouble finding a guitar in my size. I'm small and have small hands. We chose a children's guitar and shortened the neck with a capo. The capo helps. Pierre also finds me a simple method for reading notes, because I have problems with solfeggio. He adapts scores for me and writes me little things to strengthen my fingers and develop my gestures.

For the placement of my fingers, he invents funny expressions: a "two-legged spider", so that I play with two fingers, or "the spider that walks backwards", so that I climb towards the bass. We also have fun coming up with names for the pieces he invents to help me, which makes me laugh. To work on the G chord, we call the piece *Recette de sole*, like the fish.

I play Souchon's *L'Amour à la machine* and even *Les Yeux noirs,* more gypsy jazz, or blues boogie stuff like he likes. Pierre likes jazz blues and rock above all. But he lets me choose what I like best. So I'm learning to play *Belle demoiselle* by Christophe Mae, *Elle habite ici* by Gérard de Palmas or *Morgane de toi* by Renaud... I just have a few problems with tempo. I think I'm too slow.

Then I started getting interested in harder rock and pop. With my mother, we went to all the local rock concerts and festivals, and even further afield, to Brussels, Lille, Paris, Saint-Malo... At La Route du Rock, I saw The Bees, Leaves, The Notwist, Black Rebel Motorcycle Club, Suede... In Arras, I often saw Atlantys and managed to drag my mother along for Jenifer and Nolwenn Leroy.

And, of course, we're both huge fans of The Servant. We just love them. I've seen about twenty of their concerts, my mother about forty, plus the pre-concert sound checks. She's mates with Dan Black. I love the way this guy moves: like a monkey! And he has trouble saying the *u's* sometimes, like me, I've noticed that. He says "merci beaucu" in his accent.

We discovered them in February 2004, when my mother, for the release of *The Servant* album, went to Lille to interview the guitarist and singer, Chris and Dan. She recorded the concert and at the end asked them if she could put one or two songs on her Blur website. In the end, she completely redid another site on The Servant. She created the band's official fan club and a paper fanzine. Now we're buddies with the whole gang. My mother even went to London to visit Trevor, the drummer, and Chris to interview him again.

My mother and I follow them everywhere: to Châlons-en-Champagne, to the Solidays festival, to Paris-Plage, to Henin-Beaumont, to the Splendid in Lille... But we keep going to see other concerts: Sharko, Admiral Freebee, Ghinzu, Red, Dimitrios, VedeTT, Bashung... I love Bashung, especially *Osez Joséphine* and *Ma petite entreprise*. That's how I call my father's office: "How's your little business that's not in crisis?" It makes him laugh.

In November 2004, The Servant returned to Lille, at the Catho[4]. It's the ninth concert I've seen of the band since the one in May at La Cigale in Paris. I'm having the time of my life. Dan sings my favorite songs: *Jack the Ripper, Cells, Liquefy*. Generally, at concerts, I like to be in the pit to dance. As I'm small, I leave my parents behind and go right to the front. Because in a crowd, I'm crushed and suffocated. At La Catho too, I go to the front. On stage, Dan crouches down and throws his arm towards me, looking into my eyes. I know he's singing to me.

---

4. Catho is the nickname given to the Catholic University of Lille.

12. My Training

I want to earn a living. Fast. To work and have an apartment all to myself. That's why I collect internships. That's what I'm fighting for. After my internship at La Belle Époque, a retirement home in Arras where I do housework, I work in accounts at Pas-de-Calais Habitat. I do the mail registration, tax stamps, a bit of telephone work... Then I do internships at the media library and even at the Chamber of Trades. Then I was an intern at Tournant, a communications agency where my father now works.

But it was at the former Bon Secours clinic, where I was born, that I became sure of my career choice: secretarial work. But all they offered me was maintenance, catering... I wasn't interested. I don't want to work in a CAT (center d'accès par le travail) either. Besides, the lists are long. I want to work like everyone else. That's why I'm taking a BEP secretarial course and doing work-study placements.

At the beginning, for my first two-week placement, I have a little difficulty at the clinic. To put an address on an envelope, for example. I always write the address at the top left of the envelope. I'm working on this with Mrs. De Reu. We come up with a trick: I hide the part of the envelope I'm not supposed to write on with my arm, and that's it!

It was Down Up who contacted the clinic's HR department about my training. On Mondays and Tuesdays, I'm in the integration teaching unit, and on Thursdays and Fridays, at the clinic. At first, my colleagues wondered exactly what disability I had, whether they'd have to stand behind me all the time, and whether I'd be taking time away from their work. To reassure them, my department head is always present when I'm there.

Sometimes I sulk or get angry. But I soon understand who's boss. I often rehearse in the bathroom, in front of the mirror. I rehearse what I'm going to say. I need to give myself confidence. Sometimes I'm locked up for half an hour and my colleagues wonder what the hell I'm doing.

In addition to my training and internships, in 2005 and 2006, my mother and I continued to follow The Servant everywhere. At the Splendid in Lille, at the Olympia, in Cergy-Pontoise, Colmar, Cologne, Flers...

Soon, I'll know all the venues! We say hello to them at signing sessions, like at Fnac Bastille, and of course, we never miss them when they're on TV, like on *Taratata*, where they perform *Orchestra*.

Just before the Olympia concert, Matt Fisher, the bassist, gave me his hat. I was at the entrance with my mother. He said: "This is for you, Eleanor, for all the days of your life!

And then there are the other concerts: Jean-Louis Murat, Matthieu Mendès, Raphael, Amadou et Mariam, Depeche Mode...

Pierre, my guitar teacher, plays with Peter Nathanson, an American bluesman. When Nathanson came to the region in September 2006 for a concert organized at the Athies village hall, for the music center, I went too. There's an electric guitar up for grabs. I'm the "innocent hand" who has to draw a name from the hat.

I'm on stage and I pull out a piece of paper at random, and then I don't get it: I pull out my name. People look at each other, they don't understand either. I won, I'm so happy. Peter Nathanson hands me the guitar and dedicates it to me. It's a Fender Stratocaster, just my size. So Pierre and I decided to take up electric guitar and sell my other guitar.

On December 4, 2006, after two years of professional training at the clinic, I was hired. It's an eighteen-month fixed-term contract. I work twenty hours a week. It's my first real contract. I'm very happy. I have a job like everyone else. But they reduced my disability from 80% to 60%. That means I no longer get the disabled adult allowance. And that really upsets my father. He thinks they're trying to make us pay for wanting me to study and work like everyone else. So we called Vincent Potié, our lawyer, again and won.

13. My Lovers

Sometimes I don't think I'm beautiful. Some people look at me the wrong way and that hurts me. When I was operated on for my heart defect, people said, "Oh, she's not pretty to look at!" That's the main reason. It's a bit complicated to explain... When I go shopping, at the sales, I look for dresses that go all the way up to hide my scar. I don't want anyone to see it. I don't want clothes with cleavage. Swimsuits are no different. I choose swimsuits that go all the way up and hide the whole top.

But as soon as I hide it, I become beautiful. People say I'm coquettish. I like to be a bit of a tomboy, but I also like to wear dresses and skirts. I like to change my glasses. I have several pairs that I match to my outfits. And I love rocking hairstyles. I've had orange hair, red hair... My mother has already dyed her hair pink.

I had lots of boyfriends. When I was in middle school, I met Michaël. I think he was my first boyfriend... well, I'm not sure. I was 15 and he was 14. I liked his eyes and he also had a cap! I like that. He held my hand. We looked at each other. He kissed me like a savage and I was a bit embarrassed. It was in the schoolyard. We were eating together in the canteen. We had a little nothing adventure. Because in my head, I told myself that he wasn't the right boy for me: he's much too young. He talked like a young man. I dumped him.

In high school, I had two other boyfriends. Alexandre, whom I met up with again in junior high. I was already in love with him at Mrs. Bisbrouck's house. He was open and super-sympathetic to me. We talked a lot. His cool style was great, and he was calm and collected. He had Down's syndrome, unlike Michaël. I kissed him on the mouth at recess in high school, so he'd know I loved him. But he didn't think we had the right. I didn't understand why. Anyway, he was too shy. It was quick with him too.

Then I met Pierre-Alexandre. We loved each other very much. We kissed, and I'd go into his arms. I'd see him at recess. I liked his eyes, his mouth, the way he talked... everything! It lasted a long time. That was also in high school.

And then there's Robin. Robin is five years younger than me. He takes acting lessons. I'd already stopped my guitar lessons when I met him. Forty euros was becoming too expensive! Robin is very talented. He's even performed at the Comédie-Française. He played *Le Malade imaginaire* there on stage. That's when I thought: "This is the guy for me!" That was a few months before I was hired on a fixed-term contract at the clinic. I fell head over heels for him. He doesn't work like I do. So I help him find a steady job. He does internships, he looks for work.

I'm in love, just like my brother. Mathurin has just married Maïté.

I continue to enjoy concerts: The Idle Lovers, Skye, Simple Kid, Thomas Dybdahl… and in July 2007, at the Théâtre Antique de Fourvière in Lyon, I go to my twenty-sixth concert with The Servant, one month after the Showcase. They're opening for The Good, The Bad And The Queen, another band that includes Damon Albarn, whom I adore.

14. I Earn my Living

And then, in June 2008, I got my permanent contract at Arras Les Bonnettes private hospital. When the director told me the news in his office, I was overjoyed. I couldn't believe it. I feel like rubbing my hands together, as I sometimes do when I'm happy, or jumping up and down, but I want to remain professional. I'm proud of myself for finally doing it.

I write little notes to my parents, thanking them for their help. It's thanks to them that I made it. I write that I'm going to show that I'm a pro, that I'm proud of my career. And then I sign "the employee". I like to write little words of thanks and love to my parents, my brother, my friends, all the people I love. My parents have plenty of them in their desk drawers.

Mathurin works in transport logistics and I'm going to be an administrative agent for Générale de Santé d'Arras Pas-de-Calais, in the clinic's billing department. Things are going well for Mat. He and Maïté have just bought a house. As for Stephanie, a few months ago she signed her first fixed-term contract with Beaurains town council. She now works at the Louise Michel municipal library. She is in charge of checking books in and out, filing and tidying children's books, magazines...

On the day I'm hired, we celebrate my new job by eating pizza at the clinic. I make a little speech. I thank all my colleagues. I say that I'm happy to be with them and that I'll make every effort to work well. I feel well integrated in my department and there's a good atmosphere. I enjoy going to work every day.

I wake up every morning at seven twenty-five. I have breakfast: two yoghurts and an orange juice, and then I catch the 8.32 bus on line 6 to the terminus, which drops me off in front of my work. I arrive around nine o'clock, always on time or early. I start at nine fifteen.

During the Main Square festival, it's more complicated. Especially getting to work on time. It's a mess all over town and my bus has to make a huge detour to get me to work. I'm afraid of being late. It's stressing me out a bit. But it's great. There are lots of young people in the streets, with rock looks, colorful hair... Dancing everywhere, and it's right next door to me, on the Grand'Place in Arras. I'm lucky to live here. This year, it's all the rage. I see Mika in concert. The whole audience sings along to

Grace Kelly and Billy Brown. Then there's the BB Brunes, The Kooks, Sigur Rós, The Dø, Vampire Weekend and above all... Radiohead! I love all their songs, especially *Karma Police, Creep...* and also *No Surprises* and *Paranoid Android,* which they sing at the concert.

When I arrive at work at the clinic, I go over to "la Radio[5]" to see if there are any documents for the DIM (medical information department). Then I give a little kiss to all the hostesses at reception and pick up the health insurance forms. I arrive at the office I share with Isabelle. I give her a kiss, hand her the "crates[6]", undress and go round the billing colleagues to say hello and drop off the documents I've collected. I make Isa a coffee and myself a tea. That's how I start every morning. I need my big cup of tea. I sit down at my desk and start addressing.

Isabelle is more than a friend. She's almost like a second mother. I call her "ma Choupinette" and I write her little notes to tell her I love her. Sometimes, I simply say: "You know Isa, I love you".

When she's not feeling well, I see it right away. I tell her she can tell me anything. Sometimes I dream about her, that we're pampering each other and going to a little secret place in my room. I even dream about

---

5. "La Radio" is short for "Service de radiologie du center Marie Curie".
6. That's what Éléonore and her colleagues call "health insurance funds". (NdE)

14. I Earn my Living

my headmistress, that I'm touching her hair, caressing her cheek.

In the billing department, I sort mail, address and insert envelopes, do alphabetical and numerical filing, send faxes, help with reception, make photocopies and sometimes answer the phone. I even told my boss Catherine that I'd like to be a switchboard operator when I grow up. She seemed very surprised.

I take all the papers concerning my department, place them in a bin and take everything to my office. I put the regulations on one side and the prescriptions on the other. I slide the prescriptions into the "Sainte-Catherine" slot and give the regulations to another colleague. Then, for addressing and enveloping, I send invoices to patients who have paid their hospital bills. I write down the addresses of the Mutuelles and Caisses d'assurance maladie on envelopes and send them off. I'm happy to do it all.

I also sort files alphabetically, looking down to the third letter. For numerical filing, I have to look at the last three digits. To help me with the filing, Isabelle has made me a frieze with the alphabet pasted on my desk and a deck of cards so that I can practice the numerical filing. Then I note down the fax numbers and recipients on the dispatch note. I go to reception, remove the staples to put the sheets in the photocopier and send the faxes. I receive the acknowledgements of receipt and store them in separate drawers. I take care not to mix up documents.

Inserting is my favorite. I like folding invoices in thirds so that the addresses are clearly visible in the window envelopes. And alphabetical filing is great too, as it helps my memory.

At lunchtime, I have forty-five minutes to eat. Always in the canteen with my colleagues. I like to leave at noon sharp. I don't really like waiting for Isabelle, and sometimes I prefer to eat with anyone, but on time. The atmosphere is good, but I get a bit stuffy when it's busy, especially when the Red Cross students drop by. The food is good.

Isabelle keeps a close eye on what I eat. At first, she didn't dare make any comments. My first day at the clinic, we all went together to the self-service restaurant for lunch. The menu was sauerkraut. When Isabelle saw that I was taking mayonnaise, she warned me: "Careful, that's not mustard, it's mayo!" I replied, "I know," and spread it all over my sauerkraut. The girls asked me if I was used to doing that. In fact, it was my first time. At home I'm not allowed to do it, and besides, there's never any mayonnaise. So I took advantage of it.

I have to be careful because of my heart. Normally, I shouldn't weigh more than forty kilos. I find it hard to follow this advice. What's more, the canteen staff, because they like me, always serve me more. Isabelle

14. I Earn my Living

asks them to stop sometimes. She says she "looks like the bad guy". I have to limit starchy foods, avoid cheese (I love it!) and not put on weight.

Isabelle sometimes steals a dessert from me when I've got two, telling me she's still hungry. Just to see my "funny face". Afterwards, she gives it back to me, explaining that it's a joke. It doesn't make me laugh too much. When it goes on too long, I get a bit angry. Especially about the food. Isabelle says that I don't really understand jokes, that I'm "too quick to take offence" when someone makes a comment, that I take "everything at face value".

Once, a colleague, Sandrine, said to me: "Thank you, shitter". So I leave in a huff and tell Isa that Sandrine is being "dishonest" and calling me "tiotte". Isabelle explains that "tiotte" is a kind word for "little".

One day, another colleague tells me, "You're stubborn!" So I go to Isa to complain. I always confide in her. I tell her it's "mistreatment". She laughs: "Closed-minded" is not an insult. I insist. So Isabelle takes the dictionary and reads the definition: "A person of small mind, lacking intelligence". So we went to my colleague and told her we'd have to find another word. Stubborn as a donkey, for example. She agreed.

It's true that donkeys are stubborn. I've seen it with the À Petits Pas association's raids. Instead of walking, they just graze grass.

After lunch, I go back to work. I scan files and e-mail them to a colleague. On Mondays, I take stock of the files. At reception, I fold folders and sort them by color... And at ten past two, I finish. Then I go home. I'd hate to have to work like the director until nine or eleven o'clock... It tires me out!

That's my job and I really like what I do. My colleagues have become great friends. I think about them every day.

I was elected catherinette at work. It's a party where we come from, a party for little single Catherine girls. My colleagues made the hat for me out of ribbons and envelopes, and the headmistress chose me as catherinette. I was given a bouquet of roses. I started the party. I said: "And now, let's get this party started!

At the clinic, I'm treated like an adult, a colleague like any other. Isabelle takes care of me, she never talks down to me, but she's firm sometimes in her work and that's what I like. My colleagues encourage me to go further. Catherine, on the other hand, is tougher. She threatened me with a warning. That means I'm not doing my job properly, and I want to prove to her that I'm capable of doing it well. I call her "the tigress" because she gets her claws out when she's angry. But she respects me. She's polite to me like the others. She talks to me like a professional.

I want to be treated like everyone else. But sometimes I get a bit tired and I'm too slow. Like writing, which isn't really my forte! I need time. Isabelle reassures me that I make fewer mistakes than most of the trainees who've just finished their final year. I also sometimes have a bit of trouble answering the phone without stuttering, looking up zip codes in the phone book and writing them on invoices.

At first, I was bothered by the stares of people waiting in the large entrance hall. When I go to "la Radio", I also meet people who stare at me a bit sideways. It used to hurt my feelings. Now, I ignore them, I don't care.

At work, I'm sometimes called a "man-eater". Yes, I'm a bit like that. There's a trainee I really like. I've told my colleagues that I have a soft spot for him. He's an assistant in the accounts department. His name is Adrien. He's cool and collected. He takes time for me. Every time I see him, it's a pleasure. But I don't say anything out of respect for his girlfriend.

The other day, while waiting for the bus, I met a boy. His name is Sébastien. He approaches me. He tells me he wants to go out with me. Direct. So I say, "Yes". We went for a drink together. I had a little affair with him. I invite him to my place and since my parents aren't there, he comes back. My mother thinks he's very tall. He's over six feet tall.

I decide to introduce him to the clinic. I arrive one morning, hand in hand with Sébastien. I hold on to him the whole time. My colleagues are embarrassed and make funny faces. They say, "But Éléonore, who are you going out with?" They wonder. He's mentally handicapped. The others look at us from the corner and he doesn't like that. So I stopped because of the others, to get on with my life.

I enjoy going to work every day. I fought hard to get this job. I'm proud to have achieved it and, above all, to earn a living. I can't believe it! Now I feel like everyone else. I earn five hundred and eighty euros for twenty hours and with my disabled adult allowance, that makes almost one thousand one hundred euros. I'm independent. And I know that one day I'll have my own apartment.

15. Éléonore's Friends

Three months after the Dan Black concert in Tourcoing in November 2009, I received a gift from my neighbor Patrick: a canary for my future apartment. I call it "my poisoned gift", and that's what the whole family calls it now too. His real name is Baptiste. My father had to buy him a cage, and I think he regretted it a little, but it was too late. We put Baptiste on the passe-plat between the kitchen and the dining room, and it almost became Johnny's four o'clock. The cage immediately ended up on the floor: Johnny is crazy about him. So my father hung Baptiste's cage higher up on a shelf. And that's how I found poor Johnny hanging from the cage, his claws stuck. Johnny is our cat, 17 years old, which is very old for a cat. He knows how to get his claws out, but because of his age, he has trouble getting them in sometimes. As for Baptiste, he cries all day long, and my father didn't know that when we accepted the gift either. A canary isn't like a goldfish.

The following month, the Friends of Éléonore collective was created. March 25, 2010 to be exact. That's when the press really started to take an interest in us. We're in the middle of a debate on the revision of the bioethics law. There's talk of trisomy as a disease to be eradicated in PGD (pre-implantation diagnosis). Yet another stigmatization of my disease. And we're getting sick and tired of being stigmatized more and more. Instead of offering help with research and support, we're just being screened and eliminated.

My father and I are organizing a press conference to launch the collective. I'll be the spokesperson. There are sixty-five thousand people with Down's Syndrome in France and nobody hears us. It's the first time I've spoken in public, but standing next to my father, I'm no longer afraid. He explained to me what the stigma is and asked me to talk simply about myself, about how I feel as a person with Down's Syndrome. That's why he trusts me. And I know he's always proud of me.

The room is already full. There are even people sitting on the tables at the back. My father has reserved the room on the second floor of the hotel-restaurant Le Carnot, opposite the Arras train station. I sit next to him and Jean-Paul Wickart, father of Élise, with whom I went to college and who is a friend of mine. Jean-Paul is treasurer of the new association and vice-president of Down Up. I dressed up for the press conference. I wore my red tunic with a brown shawl and a top with a big white collar. My dad also looks good in his red shirt. We match. The three of us will host the press conference.

My mother, in the front row, gives me a little wave. Élise is sitting right in front of me, all quiet and intimidated. I think she's feeling a little lost in the world. I can also see Stephanie further back, Lise-Marie De Reu, and a few of my parents' friends. But I remain superconcentrated. This is an important day. I know that my father is doing all this for me too. And then I want to talk, to say things. Journalists from *La Voix du Nord*, *L'Avenir de l'Artois*, *Nord Éclair*, photographers... I don't want to say anything stupid.

My father begins. He introduces Jean-Paul and me. He talks about the revision of the law on bioethics and the advances made in research into Down's syndrome. He says that we are "full-fledged people who cannot be excluded or stigmatized", that "today we can hope to cure Down's Syndrome" and that we are a "new generation" of people with Down's Syndrome, who have had "a career in an ordinary environment", "who work, contribute and pay taxes". Then my father shows a video of me at work. He filmed me at the Sainte-Catherine clinic, before my department moved. We see my colleague Isabelle. She says that she'd never really

15. Éléonore's Friends

worked with people with Down's syndrome before she met me, and that at first she wondered what they were "going to give me to do in the billing department". Then she told me that I was "a crush" for her, that I'm "more than useful" to the department, that I'm "part of the billing team", that I'm "a full-fledged colleague, independent" in my work and that "everyone misses me" when I'm not there. Frankly, it still makes me happy to hear that, even though I'd already seen the video on my dad's computer.

I also appear in the film. I'm the one who finishes. I say words of encouragement and talk about Robin, my lover: "For Down's syndrome, you have to fight. People see people with Down's syndrome as phenomena. Down's syndrome makes a lot of people laugh, but those who make fun of me or Robin are ignored. Period. That's how I feel as a Down's syndrome sufferer. The ones who make fun of Robin... Robin has to say to himself, 'I've got more chromosomes than them!'" And then the whole room laughs, even Élise at the front.

My father takes over the microphone. He says that my testimony is "very spontaneous" and "rich", and that he wants many people to join me in the collective. Then he reminds us that my illness is stigmatized and that there is a "real danger" today with the "systematic detection of trisomy 21". Trisomy 21 must not become "the first disease stigmatized in all cases of pregnancy".

Then he gets a little angry, but I agree with him. He talks about a French family who want to work in Canada and are refused because they have a Down's syndrome child, then about an anti-Down's syndrome group on Facebook and all those who want to lock us up, hide us or put us in specialized institutions and then complain that we cost too much. It's to denounce all this that we're launching the collective and hope to gather lots of friends.

My father then reads the appeal from the Friends of Éléonore collective:

"We, the parents and friends of Éléonore, who has Down's syndrome,

We demand recognition of the dignity of all people with Down's syndrome and respect for their rights.

We refuse to allow our children and loved ones with Down's Syndrome to be discriminated against or to have their illness stigmatized.

We were dismayed by the proposal of the Conseil consultatif national d'éthique, taken up by the rapporteur of the parliamentary mission, Jean Leonetti, to extend the detection of trisomy 21 within the framework of PGD. Alternatives do exist: welcoming these people, providing information about their illness and also research into treatments that can improve their daily lives.

We refuse to accept the double penalty our children suffer: the stigmatization of the disease and the lack of public funding for research.

Our children have a right to happiness!

Today, March 25, 2010, we are launching a solemn appeal:

To all those who say yes to research rather than discrimination or stigmatization:

Join the Friends of Éléonore collective and write to us personally

to Jean Leonetti, Member of Parliament,

to deputies and senators,

to President Sarkozy,

to Prime Minister François Fillon,

to the Minister of Health and the Minister of Research,

to ask with us :

1- to fund research into a treatment for trisomy 21,

2- not to include the detection of trisomy 21, during PGD, in the draft law on the revision of bioethics laws.

Like the citizens of the Estates General on Bioethics, 'we reiterate that the solution to disability lies exclusively in research into diseases, not in their elimination'".

Everyone applauds. People ask questions. A woman, very moved, declares that she wants to help us. She looks like she's crying. Élise's father talks about research. My father explains that I want us to do a "Trisothon" because trisomy is never mentioned on the Telethon. He says I've even asked him to go to Fort Boyard to raise money, but that he's "not sporty enough for that". It makes people laugh. But I thought, since he's not very sporty, he could take part in *Who Wants to Be a Millionaire*?

Afterwards, my father said that "a ray of sunshine" like me "feels good in this world of morons". Manu, when we talk to him about stigmatization, he lets off a bit. He thinks we're not seen enough in the press, on TV... He adds that I'd also like to play in *Plus belle la vie*. It's a show I love. I watch it every day at eight fifteen.

Once, my director asked me if I'd like to go out with the actor Pascal Duquenne, who plays in *Huitième jour,* and if I'd like to make films. As for Pascal Duquenne, I said "why not", but as for the cinema, frankly, there's no doubt about it, I'd like to take Luna's place on *Plus belle la vie.* When I have to miss an episode, my mother records it. And when she goes to Australia or New Zealand for three weeks with her class, as she does almost every year, I tell her all about it. I summarize by e-mail: "Nathan has left his father. He's squatting in Ninon's apartment with a girlfriend who does the rubbish. Gaspard's father died of a heart attack. We got his ashes back", etc.

My father continues: "... And it's my neighbor who could best talk about the offence of dirty mouth!" That means it's my turn to speak, I'm *the neighbor.* I take the microphone. I'm moved and my voice is a bit shaky. I want to talk about everything that's on my mind, all the hard things we go through, all the bad things people say about us, "it's not right, it's not fair. As a person with Down's syndrome, I want to say it, it's hard. I do everything I can to fight. I explain what it's like to have a child with Down's syndrome, how I feel too… I say everything that's important to me, the love of my friends, my family, my parents… and then I start to cry. I'm so moved.

My father takes the microphone from me, but I take it back from him to continue. I thank all those who have come and then congratulate Jean-Paul and Manu and say that this collective "is a great idea". "Deep in my gut, I know it hurts, but I'm me. My mother fought hard with Dad. We've got to keep hope alive, and I want to tell Dad about Fort Boyard…" and then everyone laughs again. "As a triso, we can change everything. We can have a special Down's Telethon…". I wanted to insist on that because it's my dream.

At the end of the conference, everyone came to compliment me. My parents, who thought I'd handled my emotions well, Amandine, Lise-Marie De Reu, friends… A few days later, on the Les Amis d'Éléonore website, 1,500 people and some 30 associations signed our appeal. We also received many messages of support and congratulations. Friends, strangers, even a colleague of my mother's who chatted with Élise in the front row during the press conference.

All the regional press is talking about us: "Un chromosome en plus et pas moins épanouie[7]" (*Nord Éclair*), "Les Amis d'Éléonore vont se battre[8]" (*L'Avenir de l'Artois*), "Éléonore, 24 ans, est atteinte de trisomie 21... Et alors?[9]" (*La Voix du Nord*)... All that remains is to convince the national press.

Since the creation of the Amis d'Éléonore collective, people's attitudes have changed. People stop me in the street. They recognize me because they've seen me on TV or in the press. They congratulate me. In the street or on the bus.

My role as spokesperson for the association has helped me to move forward. Today, I want to convince mothers and doctors. I explain to them that it's possible to live with Down's Syndrome, but that a cure must be found. I used to be more shy. I'm much less shy now. It really helped when my father appointed me spokesperson for the association. I've learned to speak in public. I'm also getting out and about for World Down's Day, and I'm learning to manage my emotions with the help of my parents.

---

7. "An extra chromosome and no less fulfilled."
8. "Les Amis d'Éléonore go to battle."
9. "Éléonore, 24, has trisomy 21... So what?"

I'm very emotional. When I see my brother or another member of my family, for example. You can be emotional, but you shouldn't be for too long. Then, in my head, I say to myself: "Stop!" and I go back to the way I was before, with a smile on my face.

16. When Someone Says "Gaga" to Me

I talk to myself. That's why I feel different. I try to control myself at home in the evenings. But it's not easy. Besides, I like talking to myself. My parents asked me to avoid talking to other people. At my first two-week training course, when I was in high school, my work colleagues were shocked. They told me so.

When I was little, I used to talk to an imaginary person in the corner of a room. The doctor at Necker Hospital explained that this wasn't very good. My mother used to tell me to talk to her rather than to someone who didn't exist. I think it's part of my Down's syndrome. I still talk to myself sometimes, but discreetly and never in the street. I find it strange when people talk very loudly and alone outside. I noticed a gentleman like that.

And then I have my mimics too… I chase flies. I shake my hands, like this, to show that I'm happy. Sometimes when something's bothering me. And when I'm happy or excited about something, I rub my hands together very quickly. I avoid making these gestures in front of people.

My mother thinks I overreact.

I know I'm different, but I can't stand being infantilized.

Journalists often say to me: "And your dad… your mom…" I want people to talk to me like an adult, to say: "Your father, your mother…" I'm not a kid. I'd like to be treated like an adult. Even if I look younger. Sometimes I show press articles to my father and he exclaims, "My daughter, she's right!" It annoys my mother too when people call me "gaga". It really gets on her nerves, and I understand. One of her colleagues said to me: "Come and sit on my lap, Eleonore!" It infuriated her that people talked to me like I was 5 years old.

The cashiers at Leclerc know me and respect me. At my maternal grandmother's, whom I call *Mémé*, I was pampered. Now she's dead. I have a photo of her in my room, and every time I look at it, I hear her say, "Ah, my little girl whom I love!" That's how she spoke to me. She was affectionate, but at the same time she gave me a boost. She'd make me a big bowl of hot chocolate with big snacks. I'd say, "Thank you, Grandma," and she'd say,

"You're welcome, my little girl, whom I love." Every time I went to her house, I'd watch Robuchon's cooking show with her, then *C'est mon choix* with Évelyne Thomas and then my TV series... She never infantilized me either. She never did. She talked to me like she would anyone else. Not like my paternal grandmother, who's just affectionate. I like to be pushed to do interesting things, but she talked to me like a kid. But she also talks like that to my father... She says things like: "My son was handsome when he was young. My son this, my son that..." It bothers me.

My paternal grandparents are very religious. They go to mass every Sunday, at midday, at midnight... They also go to Lourdes. They say they pray for me there, I don't know why. I was baptized to please them, but then I stopped. I didn't take communion. God, Jesus, all that... It's not my thing, I don't really care. I don't believe in them. I think it's a waste of time. My mother is an atheist. And even more so since Valentin's death. Don't bother her with religion! She was baptized and even made her communion. But when she was 14, she decided to stop going to church. Anyway, she didn't listen to the priest, she went with her school books, her English books. That's how she became an English teacher. Her parents gave up. My mother says you can be a good person without religion. And my mother is a good person. My dad's like her, but he's calmer about

16. When Someone Says "Gaga" to Me

the whole thing. I think that's why my paternal grand-mother used to call me "gaga". Because of God.

People like me. They tell me I'm kind, affectionate, smiling... and that touches me. It's only people who don't know me who call me "gaga".

17. A Collective that's Making a Splash

After the creation of the collective, everything accelerated. On April 30, my father and I left for Rennes. And we really didn't have time to visit the city. We immediately had to prepare the press conference, the tables, the chairs, the projector... After Arras, we were starting to get the hang of it. The presentation, the questions, the journalists...

On May 7, we go down to Marseille. My father asks me if I'm ready to speak again. I think about what I'm going to say. And again, everything goes well. The audience is nice. But this time we had a little more time, and the next day I asked to visit the *Plus belle la vie* studios.

I make my dad walk all over town, and I think it's really funny. Plus, he drags our suitcases. "Do you

really want to see the *Plus belle la vie* studios, darling?"
He kept asking me that because he was fed up with us
going round in circles. We couldn't find the Belle de
mai studios. I don't care, I love walking. "Of course
I do, Dad!" We walked and walked... And when we
found the studios, we saw barriers everywhere. We
couldn't get in. All we could see was the window of the
Bar du Mistral.

Later in the day, on France Info, Marie Christine
Lauriol, correspondent in Marseille, talked about us:
"Les Amis d'Éléonore stopped off in Marseille yesterday
[...]. Created on March 25 by parents and relatives of
people with Down's syndrome, the group has embarked
on a tour of France to call on the French government
to fund research into this disease [...]. Today, the only
proposal made to parents is screening and diagnosis
[...]. On the eve of the Health Minister's presentation
of the draft revision of the bioethics laws, the legislator
is even considering creating a list for pre-implantation
diagnosis, in which trisomy 21 would be the only one
to appear. If this law were adopted, trisomy 21 would
become the first disease to be stigmatized..." And then
the channel talks about welcoming people with Down's
Syndrome, providing information about the disease,
finding treatments...

On May 20, we're in Paris. Élise and her father,
Jean-Paul, join us. A journalist from Le *Pèlerin* and

a photographer follow us all day. We headed for the Ministry of Health. We're due to meet Minister Roselyne Bachelot. In fact, it's one of her advisors who receives us, Alain Graf, rapporteur for the Estates General on Bioethics. I'm impressed by him, because he's huge and very serious. He listens and takes notes when we talk about the collective. As for Manu, he's disappointed not to see the Minister. Mr Graf says that Roselyne Bachelot doesn't want to put Down's syndrome on the list of diseases to be eradicated, and that's what we want. But when we go out, we don't really know what to think. My father says, "We'll see." We've got a bit of time to take a trip to the Trocadero, see the Eiffel Tower and then discuss what we're going to say in the restaurant. Then it's off to the Hôtel de la Bourdonnais for the press conference. I'm happy because among the audience I find my godmother, who lives not far away, in Neuilly, and who has come to see me.

But the day's not over yet. We're off to see Jean-Paul Delevoye, the French Ombudsman. He's oversized, like his office. Everything is neat and tidy, with pencils, a diary and bodyguards. Jean-Paul Delevoye has known my father since he was a child, and even my paternal grandparents. He's mayor of Bapaume. It's about ten kilometers from Moyenneville where Manu was born.

Élise is even more shy than usual and I find myself very small next to Jean-Paul. I tell him I'm right on

17. A Collective that's Making a Splash

his shoulder. He replies that it's no problem and bends down to kiss me. I really like him. He's like a friend to me.

The same day, the Public Sénat channel broadcast a report about me. In it, my father recounts our morning meeting with Alain Graf. Senator Bernadette Dupont was a guest on the set. She has a Down's syndrome daughter. Then comes another report, the 12:45 presented by Aïda Touihri on M6, shot two days earlier in Arras. We see me at home, on the bus, at work... my life told in less than three minutes: "Her name is Éléonore, and according to the doctor who gave birth to her, she was a chromosomal aberration, in other words, a Down's syndrome sufferer. Twenty-four years later, the 'aberration' is a fulfilled woman. Today, she works like everyone else, and her challenge now is to fight on behalf of people with Down's syndrome. This morning, she was received by the Minister of Health..." I look great in the film, wearing my striped leggings under a short tartan skirt. Very rock!

The press is also talking about us: *La Croix, France Soir, La Vie, Le Parisien...* "Éléonore s'en va-t-en guerre[10]", "Éléonore, trisomique, ne veut pas du dépistage de sa maladie[11]", "Une jeune trisomique fait entendre sa voix

---

10. "Éléonore goes to war."
11. "Éléonore, with Down's syndrome, doesn't want to be screened for her condition."

dans le débat bioéthique[12]", "Éléonore ou le droit au bonheur[13]", etc.

On May 22, we received a visit from an advisor to Prime Minister François Fillon. David Gruson is an advisor on health issues. He's originally from Arras. He comes to chat with my parents at home before rejoining his family.

May 27 is the France Télévision symposium on integrating disabled people into the workplace. In the morning, *Arras Actualités* takes a photo of us in front of the TGV, a few hours before the conference where my father is due to speak. This time, I stay in the audience. The next day, my photo appeared in an article entitled "Pour que toutes les Éléonore ont droit de cité" ("So that all Éléonores have a right to be heard"). The journalist points out that when parents are told they have trisomy 21, "92% of cases result in systematic elimination of the foetus".

On June 24, France 3 Nord Pas-de-Calais reports. "Should screening for trisomy 21 be made systematic?" Here, I'm seen with my colleague Isa and my parents. My father explains that you can live with someone with Down's syndrome and be happy with them. My mother was very moved in the report and I wanted to support

---

12. "A young Down's syndrome patient raises her voice in the bioethics debate."
13. "Éléonore or the right to happiness."

her when she talked about my birth while looking at my photos. Catherine Genisson appeared on the channel after the report. She's part of the parliamentary mission that worked on the bioethics law. I really like this woman. She's nice, not very tall like me, and she supports us.

On July 7, Manu and Jean-Paul Wickart meet Jean Leonetti in his office at the French National Assembly. I thank him for receiving us. My father explains why the Friends of Eleonore collective was set up, talks about the stigma, the need for funding for research, and the collective's actions. Jean Leonetti says there will be no list of diseases for PGD, but he wants parents to be informed about screening. He's afraid parents will sue afterwards. He dedicates a book to me: *Quand la science transformera l'humain.* He writes: "For Éléonore who knows that… when science transforms the human… we must preserve the fragility of the human. Kind regards."

Two days later, we received a reply from Minister Roselyne Bachelot, dated July 7. It was sent to us by Jean-Pierre Kucheida, Member of Parliament. She wrote: "It has been indicated to the Friends of Éléonore collective that I will pay particular attention, when the bioethics law is re-examined, to maintaining the current provisions, which reserve the indication of pre-implantation diagnosis for incurable and particularly serious diseases, of which trisomy 21 is not one." On

December 15, 2010, Thierry Berthou, the photographer, followed me around all day to prepare the book *Supplément d'âme*. A book of fourteen portraits: people with Down's syndrome and then a few others, like the writer Jean-Louis Fournier or the lawyer Vincent Potié, who fought alongside my parents to keep me in school. Stephanie and Robin will be in the book too. Thierry photographs me at home, with my electric guitar, in front of my mirror, then accompanies me to work.

During the bus ride, a guy gets angry and says, "Stop taking my picture!" So Thierry says what he's doing and explains that he's interested in me. The man calmed down.

In the afternoon, we speak and debate in Paris with members of parliament and the philosopher Danielle Moyse at the National Assembly. He follows me again. While waiting in a café outside the Assemblée Nationale, I spot David Douillet. I go to see him to talk judo and Thierry takes my photo with him.

Now that there's the collective, I have a little less time to go to concerts. But I didn't want to miss Gorillaz's *Escape to Plastic Beach* tour. I was able to go and see them on November 25, at the Lotto Arena in Antwerp, with my mother and Mathurin.

I love this third album, *Plastic Beach*. The whole Damon Albarn clique was there: Bobby Womack, Neneh Cherry, Simon Tong, Mick Jones and Paul Simonon from the Clash... We were up high, we could see the whole stage and the eight thousand people around. It was gigantic!

I was blown away by the opening song, then Snoop Dogg on the giant screen, the *Stylo* video with Bruce Willis, Bobby Womack's *Cloud of Unknowing* and his impressive voice. And Bashy and Kano were too good in *Clint Eastwood* and all those Jamie Hewlett cartoons... For me, it's the concert of the year.

18. The Islet of Bon Secours

The Sainte-Catherine clinic has moved to the Arras Les Bonnettes hospital. This is the second move in my job since the Bon Secours clinic.

Manu thinks the Bon Secours clinic should be transformed. He dreams of an "inter-generational residence". I wrote the word down in one of my repertoires. It means mixing all ages. My father often talks about that when he explains his project.

But right now, it's a real mess! It's all white and empty. It's a bit sad. He works with the Pas-de-Calais Habitat social landlord where I did my internship. He tells me that they have fond memories of me there, especially Martine, my internship tutor. He's preparing the residence with Down Up and a seniors' association. He's been working on it for three years, ever since he heard the clinic was up for sale. The residence will be called "l'îlot Bon Secours".

More than ten years ago, my father and Pas-de-Calais Habitat wanted to create an artistic factory for people with intellectual disabilities. Leroy Merlin agreed to be their partner. But as the associations working with the disabled didn't agree, he stopped. Now, with Bon Secours, it's going to work.

The clinic was rebuilt and the landlord kept the chapel and opened a company crèche for thirty children. Manu reviewed the plans and with other architects, they changed a few things. At first, they didn't realize that we were so small compared to the other people with Down's syndrome. So they had to change the height of the intercoms. On the doors, they added a second peephole, lower down, because I couldn't see anything. My father also wanted Italian-style showers, flush with the floor, and open kitchens with practical ovens: the doors slide underneath so you don't burn yourself, and induction hobs, rather than gas, which he found too dangerous. He also wanted wheelchairs to be able to go everywhere, as well as communal spaces where people could meet up, a hanging garden... The Bon Secours island is big. I go there from time to time with my father to see how the work is progressing. It's all white and there's no furniture or decor yet.

There are seventy-five apartments. Ten are for people with Down's syndrome. My parents told me that's where I'm going to live. I don't know when, but I'm happy.

When my brother got an apartment, I thought: "So why not me?" I won't have my parents around anymore, as I said on TV. I'm going to be independent at last. I've been dreaming about my apartment, my bedroom, my office... with bright colors everywhere.

I'm getting an apartment, but my brother is going to sell the house he bought with Maïté two years ago. Things aren't going very well between them. They've split up. Maïté met a girl. I think Mat doesn't know how to think and still hopes she'll come back.

19. What is Love?

I broke up with Robin because he didn't have a job. And then there was another thing that irritated me too much: his over-protective mother. He was always up her skirt! I'm not like that. Robin and I are buddies. He's like a brother to me. But I went back to Benjamin.

I met Benjamin in high school when I was 20. He's now 24. He's not triso, but he has an intellectual disability. His story is… a bit complicated. He has serious problems with his father. Every time I see him on the bus, he makes a fuss. He keeps telling Benjamin to stop seeing me. He's lost his wife, his job, so he's taking it out on his son. He says "that girl" shouldn't go out with his son, because I've got Down's Syndrome. He doesn't like that at all.

In early February 2011, TF1 came to film me for the show *C'est quoi l'amour?* Three of them came to Arras for the report. Lucienne the journalist, Adrien the cameraman and Denis the soundman. They've set up in the center of town, at the Ibis hotel, and they're going to stay three days for me, to follow me everywhere.

Benjamin and I are filming in the streets of Arras. We're window-shopping for Valentine's Day, just the two of us, as lovers. We want to buy each other little gifts. I go into *La Carterie* to buy her a Valentine's Day card with funny cats. We exchange love notes.

At first, Benjamin's father agreed to let his son be interviewed, but he didn't understand that it was being filmed. So, afterwards, he refused to let us see his son on TV, especially with me. He talks loudly with Lucienne on the phone, and also with my father. TF1 offers to blur Benjamin, but the father doesn't even want to see his son blurred! He threatens Manu and wants to press charges. I intervene: "Dad, we're going to stop this right now, because it's creating problems and it's going to fall on Benjamin." So Benjamin was removed from the film.

I was really sad and so was Benjamin. On the other hand, my brother agreed to be filmed, and that made me very happy. It's the first time. It was for lunch at home. We're eating andouillettes and Mat explains why our parents spent more time with me when we were little.

I love andouillette. We buy it at Becquart's and when I go there, he always gives me a slice of garlic sausage, because he likes me. My mother tells me that he never gives her anything. What's more, he makes crépinettes and tripe… I love it! In Arras, there's also the andouillette festival on the Grand'Place. It's held every August 25, the day before my birthday. We don't go, but on all my birthdays we eat andouillette.

After dinner, I showed the TF1 team my room, with my photos and posters from The Servant, and then my notebooks and my dictionary, the big Robert Collège. They filmed me again the next day: in the morning for breakfast, at home, in the bathroom when I was doing my hair, then on the bus.

People often look at me sideways on the bus. "It hurts me, it makes me feel like I've been stabbed." That's what I say in the report. And then we go to my job. At Générale de Santé management, they're getting a bit fed up with journalists. They've already seen France 3, M6, *La Voix du Nord…* They say it's a bit disruptive to the service, but they still accept it.

At home, TF1 films me looking at photo albums with my parents. My mother talks about my birth. She's very moved, and so are the TV crew. She confides that if she'd known I had Down's syndrome, she might have had an abortion, if the doctors had told her it was for the best, but she's glad she didn't know. I tell her that "I fought to live". "From the moment you were born, you started fighting to live," Mum repeated.

Today, it's even worse. Mothers are forced to know. It must be hard for them to make a choice. My dad says it's sad when the world chooses who is born. On my Mac, I have lots of videos of mothers talking about the birth of their child with Down's syndrome. Manu filmed them for Down Up. They feel abandoned and lost. Sometimes we don't explain anything to them, or we ask, "What do you want to do with it?"

With the TF1 team, we go to DanjouBoda and I choose the colors for my kitchen: green and red. Vibrant colors just the way I like them. Then we go to see the work on the Bon Secours island. I visit the apartment where I'll be living. This is when I really realize that this is my home. It's absolutely splendid! I'll have forty-eight square meters. It's great, but there's still work to be done! My father asks me if I want a single or double bed. I say, "Double, in case my boyfriend comes over.

My parents are worried that I'll soon be on my own, so I reassure them that I'll be able to spend weekends with them and that I'll buy some beers for my father. He likes Ch'ti and Rince Cochon. I can't wait to live at home now, to be like my brother.

Several weeks later, I take the TGV to record *C'est quoi l'amour?* Someone was waiting for us at the station and we took a cab to the studios. It's in a very large hangar. They do my hair and makeup. I like it, because it makes me feel more like a woman. They bring us drinks. The technical team is very nice. I even took photos with Carole Rousseau. Frankly, she's worth it, she's superb!

She asks me what I want to do with my lover. So I tell her I want an engagement, my bachelorette party, my Down's syndrome party and marriage. During the show, she asked me if my parents' demands were difficult at times. I replied: "That's a good question. In two months, I'll have my own place and I want to tell them, give me a break!"

20. My Home

I like to go home on Sunday evenings. When I arrive, I take off my coat, put on my slippers and put my suitcase in my room. Today, I can manage my life on my own. What's more, I can cook, sort my laundry, check my mail, do my accounts, empty my dishwasher, do my housework... My parents are messy, a bit like Stephanie. I'm tidy. I like my home to be spotless.

Yes, that's it! I've moved in! I live on the fourth floor, where the old maternity hospital used to be, in the prefecture district of Arras. It's where I was born and where I did my first internships. It was on the first floor. I think I've already told the story.

The first night I slept alone at home, I was happy and excited. I had my own place, just like my brother. I was a little scared too. When my parents said "Bye, Éléonore" and I replied "Hi, lovers", I found myself alone behind the door and it felt really strange. I was also impressed to be on the fourth floor. When I looked out of the window, I felt a bit dizzy. I was really high up. At night, I dreamt of myself alone in the apartment and my parents living out their lives as a couple. I was independent. In the morning, my parents called to see if everything had gone well. There were one or two weekends that I preferred to spend at home. Now, I really enjoy being with my parents every Friday evening. For four hours a week, I have a carer who comes to help me with my clothes and meals. One of them talked to me a bit like a kid at first, so I told her she could talk to me normally. Now she respects me and talks to me like everyone else, like an adult.

I chose bright colors everywhere. Red and green for my kitchen, pink and green for my bathroom. With my parents, I bought three chandeliers, one red, one pink and one orange, a purple wooden desk and a red sofa. Here, I have my books, my guitar, a photo of Mathurin as a field hockey player in my kitchen, Matt Fisher's beige hat by my bed, an autographed photo of Carole Rousseau on my bookshelf, and, above my desk, a photo taken in The Servant's dressing room in 2007, at Le Splendid in Lille, just after the concert. Dan and Matt and I play the fool. Dan is wearing one of the T-shirts he had painted that afternoon.

On the other hand, I left my "poisoned gift" in its cage at my parents' house. It's bad enough I let my plants die...

My rent is three hundred and sixty euros, but as I receive APL (aide personnalisée au logement), I pay very little. I'm starting to do my own accounts. I look at my expenses on the Internet and transfer them to my accounts. When my father saw my notebook, he said to me: "But you're in the red, my darling!" I'd written down my expenses, but I'd forgotten to include what I earn from my job and my disabled adult allowance.

At home, I watch less and less TV. Mostly I listen to music, French pop and rock. Mostly rock. Depeche Mode, Gossip... and I play electric guitar. Now I'm back at school with a new teacher, François-Xavier. I go to Art & Music every Wednesday. That's where Stephanie takes her painting lessons. It's a group class. The others play harmonica or ukulele. I play songs by Bob Dylan, Gossip, Adèle or the Rolling Stones. I also like this band. Three years ago, I went to see Scorsese's *Shine a Light* about the Rolling Stones. Keith Richards is my buddy. He's my favorite, with his pirate face. Right now, I'm working on *Rolling in the Deep*. I'll have to show Robin, he loves singing Adèle. He also lives in the residence, as does Stephanie. Everyone I love.

Everyone in the residence can meet up at the Kiosque, in the conviviality room. There are elderly people, triso people like me and young families too. That was my father's idea: to bring everyone together and create a kind of small village.

In the early days, Stephanie, Robin, Amandine and the others ran the Kiosque. We'd make little coffees for the elderly. After a while, we got fed up of serving them and seeing them wait without doing anything. Now, we play board games, chat... And we make them coffees if we want, just to be nice. I go to the Kiosk because I need to see people. There's a good atmosphere with the people in the residence.

Old people are a little slower than we are. To walk, to think, but not to talk. Sometimes they get tired, so they go home and take a nap. It reminds me of my maternal grandmother. Before she died, I used to help her eat too. We'd take her out in a chair and she'd be so happy.

Here I find Gertrude. She's an old lady. She's 88 years old. I like her a lot. She has a son in Gabon and a daughter, Betty, who works with me at the clinic as a midwife. She also has a little girl, Léna. Gertrude always talks to me like an adult. She talks to me a lot about her children. When she comes to the Kiosk, she always drops in to see how I'm doing. She was even filmed with Stephanie and me. It was for Claire Chazal's 8 o'clock news. She confided that she saw Stéph' and me as her great-grandchildren. She's doing well, Gertrude. She has her hair appointments, her dentist appointments, she does her shopping... There's also Monique, another elderly person. Monique doesn't say anything and I don't know anything about her. I talk to her and she listens to me.

Pascale and Philippe are the neighbors of Célia, another friend with Down's syndrome whom I love dearly. Pascale was on France 2 with me. She comes to the Kiosk sometimes. She often takes care of Célia. She told me that if I have a hard time, I can come and see her. But I've never stopped by. She's very interested in Down's syndrome.

Amandine also has Down's syndrome. She works at Foyer Soleil, a retirement home. She looks after the elderly, prepares meals for them and makes them laugh. She even danced for them once. She's nice and she does really funny things. On the other hand, when she's in a bad mood, we ignore her with the other friends. She's very sporty. She runs cross-country at Simencourt, and at home, she sings karaoke to Lorie and Garou. Amandine dresses any way she wants. She pulls her tights up to her navel. She goes bare-armed when it's cold and long-sleeved when it's hot. She mixes everything up and wears big socks with pantacourts... In my opinion, she has a problem with the weather.

Mario also has Down's Syndrome and diabetes. He is tested before eating to make sure he doesn't have too much sugar in his blood, and a nurse comes to see him.

He mustn't take anything too sweet. I like sweet things, but I don't want to end up like him. Mario is 23 years old. He plays the piano and every morning when I cross the corridor to go to work, I hear him. He plays superbly. It puts me in a good mood. He goes to the speech therapist like me and to his piano class at the conservatory, all by himself, on his cab bike. He's in love with Amandine. He's sweet, but sometimes a little aggressive. The other day, I was clearing the table and he snatched the salt shaker out of my hand. He's a bit nervous.

When we do the Fête de la musique downstairs in the hanging garden, Mario plays the piano. I play the electric guitar, which we plug in with an extension lead in the social room, and Robin plays the flute. Mario also practices with Mrs. Sarrazin, another 90-year-old lady who lives at the residence. She offered to help him on the piano.

Christian is the residence's maintenance man. He's employed by Logista. He washes the entrance floors, the corridors... and repairs everything. He's the one you call when you have a problem: a fire alarm going off, a missing seal on the front door or a water leak in the shower. He's kind and helpful. He also comes to see us at the newsstand. Sometimes I check on his daughter, who plays soccer.

There's also Geneviève, an old lady who likes to come down to the nursery and tell stories to the children.

Sometimes we pay each other little visits. We invite each other over for aperitifs.

At first, it was a party in the residence. But frankly, it was a bit of a mess. People were running around in their pajamas at all hours. We'd have pizza parties. Mario would knock on his neighbor's door at night when he wanted waffles... So we talked it over with Mrs. Bisbrouck, my old high school teacher. She's the one who comes to lead the Down Up discussion groups, along with Gaëlle, our educator.

We, Mrs. Bisbrouck, just call her "Madame", but those who don't know her like we do, call her "Elisabeth".

She created the Down Up tenants' committee. It was with her that we decided that each floor would have its own manager. I'm in charge of the whole fourth floor. And now, I've become president of the committee. That's why I wrote the rules on my computer and presented them to the committee. I'm like my father: we have to keep moving forward!

At our tenants' meeting, we set some rules: no running in the corridors, no visiting each other after 8.30pm, respect for the carers... But we can still invite each other in and see each other even later, like on Saturday night. And we said we'd change the rules afterwards, when everyone has calmed down.

Every day, I have activities and appointments to keep after work. On Mondays, it's gentle gymnastics, and on Tuesdays, it's the Kiosk from 3 p.m. to 5 p.m. in the social room. I also go there on Thursday afternoons. On Wednesdays, I have my electric guitar class. On Thursdays, I see my speech therapist, and then I have my Down Up discussion group. On Fridays, I go to the physiotherapist.

Mrs. Bisbrouck explains that the discussion group is not for settling weekly scores or private matters. We should only talk about things that concern the group. Right now, we're talking about rights and duties, responsibility and self-determination. Sometimes, Mrs. Bisbrouck comes up with a question: "What if everyone did what they wanted?" So we say whatever we'd like to do. But Mrs. Bisbrouck wants us to talk more about the group. So the following week, she asked us, "What if everyone did anything, anyhow, anywhere?" And then we had a good laugh, because we could say anything too.

21. Open House

I don't have to leave people on the doormat anymore. That's what Gaëlle, our educator, explained to me, because that's what I used to do when I received people in my home. I used to forget to say to people: "Come in!" So they'd stay outside. Even my parents expect me to say, "Come in, lovers!" Now, I'm careful.

When I offer my guests a drink, I also have to ask them what they want before serving them orange juice. Gaëlle, for example, likes clementine juice, and sometimes she prefers tea.

Today, there are lots of people. They're milling around in the residence corridors. I tell them, "You can come in now!" My father wasn't expecting so many people this morning. It's October 8, 2011, the open house for the Bon Secours block. I have to show people around my apartment, as do Amandine, Robin, Stéph' and the other Down Up tenants.

At home, I'm comfortable and everything's fine. It's been three months since I moved in. Stephanie, for her part, gave a floral art presentation with her mother in her apartment. Robin, who shares his apartment with Pierre-Alexandre, laid out cakes, a *libouli* tart and brioche for people passing by. As for Thibaut, he has decorated everything in the colors of the UK flag, from coasters to toilet lids! He did all the decorating. Mario plays the piano at home and offers chicory leaves with tuna mayonnaise. His parents grow chicory. My mother says they taste nothing like greenhouse chicory!

I made myself beautiful. I put on the little blue top I like. The one with the long sleeves that come up to my hands and I slip on by the thumb, like a glove. It's so stylish. I'm also wearing black tights, a purple cardigan and a colorful necklace and hair.

Manu makes a short speech in the downstairs room to introduce the residence. He also talks about the book *Supplément d'âme*, which came out a month ago. There's a cocktail party, croissanterie, charcuterie... On the fourth floor, I show my apartment to everyone who passes by: people from Arrage whom I've never seen, others I've met before, but also a few people I know, like Lise-Marie De Reu, my former IT teacher, Fleur and her mother, cousins, my godmother Bernadette and my father's parents...

I act as a guide. I show them my kitchen with its pantry, my retractable oven door, my living room with my TV, my CDs, my Freebox, my bedroom-office... People leave me nice messages in my guest book, congratulating me on my apartment. They write that it's "lovely and colorful like [me]" and wish me "happiness for [my] new life".

Jean-Paul Delevoye also comes to visit my apartment. Élise follows him. While he signs my visitors' book, I put on the cap he'd given me with the name of the town where he's mayor: "Ville de Bapaume". It makes him laugh, and I clap my hands like a rapper. For him, I give him the full tour, including my kitchen, my oven, my view of the hanging garden... Journalists follow us and take notes or photos of Jean-Paul or my oven.

Around noon, we leave for lunch at the Carnot. I get into Jean-Paul Delevoye's car. That's when he asks me if he can talk about all of us in his speech, even Valentin, my dead little brother. I don't mind. We also talk about it sometimes at home, when we look at our baby photos from the maternity ward. We join my parents, my godmother Bernadette, Mathurin and a friend of his, Florian. At the table, Jean-Paul Delevoye is a little bored with my godmother, so he chats the whole meal with Mat's friend. They get along great.

The day continues at the town hall, at the belfry, in the Salle d'Honneur, for the presentation of Manu's medal. It's a superb room lined with a huge canvas depicting medieval peasants and merchants holding pigs and geese in the squares of Arras.

I give the first speech. Only my mother knows it, because I asked her to help me type it on the Mac. Jean-Paul Delevoye gives me the floor, then remembers something: "Ah, excuse me, we need a little set-up" and leaves to find a stool so that I can be seen a little better behind the microphones, because I'm small. I welcome everyone, my family and "my girlfriends up front". Then I start reading my speech:

"Dad, I'm so proud of you. You always go out of your way to make things happen for us.

Every Tuesday, after lunch, you go to your Down Up meeting. You're not home, but I know you do this for me and you do it well. I'm proud to be the president's daughter.

Dad, you're obviously working hard for the Friends of Éléonore collective. When you talk about the bio-ethics law and the non-stigmatization of trisomy 21, I fight with you. You know I'm proud of you.

Manu, congratulations on creating the Bon Secours block project.

I was born at the old Bon Secours clinic, I did my first internships in the clinic's billing department and now I have my apartment here.

The Bon Secours islet is a great idea.

Thanks to you, we have beautiful kitchens that we've chosen at Danjou.

Thanks to you, we have household help, which is great.

We also have iPhones and iPads so we can see each other and get help.

The project is progressing well. That's what I like about you, when you do something, you see it through to the end.

Manu, I also congratulate you on the book *Supplément d'âme* pour changer le regard.

You've earned your medal. Manu, my hat's off to you." My father is moved and I think he liked it when I talked about the kitchens. It made him laugh a little. He kisses me and congratulates me. I say to my parents: "Kiss each other, lovers!" Jean-Paul Delevoye takes the microphone in his turn and begins a beautiful, lengthy speech, in which he recounts the life of the whole family. He recalls my father as a young man, when he was working, at the age of 15, and how he and Mom met in high school. I think Manu was in first grade, but I'm not sure. My mother fell in love with him at first sight. She wanted to be an English teacher and went to the United States for a year when she was 18. And there she fell in love again, with Bob Dylan. Jean-Paul doesn't talk about it, but I do.

Then he talks to my grandparents, who are here too. They wanted my father to be a priest. They didn't care. My father wanted to study Fine Arts. Instead, he spent two years in the minor seminary and a month in a psychiatric hospital in the army. And he never told me that. Jean-Paul also tells us that Manu used to sell Indian ink drawings in front of the Monoprix in Arras, where I was spanked. But I guess I wasn't born yet. Jean-Paul goes on to talk about the Beaux-Arts in Paris, while Maryse, my mother, does housework and a master's degree in English... Then he talks about Mathurin, Valentin, me, my health problems...

At the end, I bring him the medal on a little red cushion and Jean-Paul, right in front of Manu, declares in a big voice: "In the name of the President of the Republic and by virtue of the powers vested in us, we make you a knight in the Order of Merit." I've never seen my brother so moved. Everyone applauds, everyone embraces and everyone heads for the buffet prepared by the Lycée hôtelier de Saint-Charles. You can sample charcuterie, *Potjevleesch,* maroilles, coeur d'Arras, mimolette, tomme de Cambrai, *tarts al'suc* and drink Page 24 and lemonade.

The following month, I was again featured in several reports, on France 3 Nord Pas-de-Calais, Laurent Delahousse's 13 heures on France 2... And then I was on the radio, on Vivre FM with my father. Christophe

Bougnot interviews us. He's calm and cool. He talks to me normally. He asks me questions that other people don't ask me. He asks me about my reading, my future, the clichés about people with Down's syndrome being seen as children... I reply that "I already feel like an adult". I tell him about my Down's syndrome, "which is visible, it's true", and about the "mockery and mistreatment" that are "not good memories". I explain my idea for a Down's Telethon... because it's close to my heart.

22. Célia

Célia is one of the first residents of the Bon Secours block. She's also a friend. I've known her since the Jura. That's where we went to Bois-d'Amont, with the Geist 62 association. That was in February 1996. I was still in CE2. It's also where I learned to ski with Fleur and Stephanie. That's why Célia always says that I'm her "childhood friend". Is that all she knows how to say? Frankly, it gets on my nerves sometimes!

Célia moved in with Laurence in May 2011. Of the ten apartments reserved for people with Down's Syndrome, two were intended as shared apartments. The aim was to make life easier for younger people like Robin and Laurence. At least, that's what everyone thought. It wasn't that simple... My father says that "it was a bit of a failure". In fact, it was a disaster!

The people had to get along, but so did their families. Gilles-Emmanuel was supposed to live with Célia, but when that didn't work out, Laurence took his place and let him have his apartment. As a result, Célia and Laurence moved in together. A little later, Robin and Pierre-Alexandre moved into the second apartment, which was meant for two people. Robin ended up alone. Pierre-Alexandre had plenty of internships away from Arras. And when he failed his CAP, his mother decided he should move. She ran a specialized establishment. Maybe she didn't think the residence was good enough for her son.

I think it's great that Robin lives alone. Besides, I can see him at home, in peace and quiet.

Célia was 29 when she arrived at l'îlot Bon Secours. She was working in an ESAT (establishment and service for the disabled) and living in an apartment outside Arras, alone. She didn't see many people, between her job and her apartment. So she was happy to meet up with Laurence. Laurence is younger: she's eight years younger. The two girls got on really well. They fell in love with each other, and that's when they started their bullshit...

They were sometimes angry with their families. They didn't like being separated at weekends either. So they decided to go off on their own. That was in December 2011, the same month I saw the Prime Minister, François

Fillon, to talk about the collective, ask for funding for research and propose that Down's Syndrome become a major national cause. Anyway, it all came to nothing. In short, Laurence and Célia decided to leave. My father calls the story "one hell of a lesson in autonomy". Nevertheless, he panicked like the others when he heard about the runaway. It was over the phone. He was with me and my mother at my guitar teacher's concert. Laurence and Célia's parents hadn't found their daughters and had imagined the worst.

It was panic. That evening, my father and the girls' parents searched the whole of Arras. Laurence's father went to the gendarmerie to report his daughter missing, but as he was pretty drunk, the gendarmes made him blow into the balloon and confiscated his license, straight away.

Célia and Laurence had withdrawn money from an ATM and gone for a romantic dinner at a pizzeria. They had also booked a small two-star hotel near the belfry on Place des Héros in Arras for the night: the Hotel Diamant. They had unplugged their phones to stay off the grid. The next day, they had spent the whole day shopping in peace and quiet.

Eventually, one of the girls used her phone, and that's how they were found, the day after they disappeared. The parents weren't happy. My father was furious, but he looked for a solution in the residence and proposed other apartments. But Laurence's parents refused. They wouldn't listen. They preferred to take their daughter home for three or four months. They almost locked her up and found her another apartment near Bon Secours.

It's a very sad story. The girls were punished and their parents never spoke to each other again. Anyway, Celia's father is a psychiatrist in La Réunion and Laurence's father drinks a lot and has separated from his wife. The girls still love each other, but no longer see each other.

I'm still seeing Célia around the residence. Today, she works at La Finarde, the citadel's cheese dairy. She's very close to me. She confides in me a lot, because she's having a hard time coping with her parents' divorce. I explained to her that Laurence had manipulated her and treated her like an object.

My father says Celia's not the girl for me. As soon as I mention her to my parents, they get upset. They think I'm too suggestible.

The other day, I spent the evening with Celia and we kissed on the mouth. The next day, my father asked me why I was so tired. I'd gone to bed at three in the morning. I explained. My father wasn't happy. Now I only see Celia outside. I prefer it that way. It's a rule I made. I also told her mother.

Celia's in love with me and I think she's delusional. She's fixated on me. I'm not in love with her. She's a friend, but sometimes I can't keep up with her and

I have to make cuts. I keep my distance. But I like the way she looks at me, the way she talks to me. I dreamt she was kissing me again.

Once, my father was filming at the Journées de la science in Paris, for the Fondation Jérôme Lejeune. It was a few years ago. I explained to him on camera that I was a lesbian: "Men aren't for me. I like women, they interest me." But I talk to my mother about it. She thinks that's why I love Beth Ditto, the singer from Gossip. She's a lesbian too, and strong like Celia. She's kind of my role model.

When I hear Soan's song, *Inch alleluia, I* think of Célia. I feel like dedicating it to her. Her words touch me. That's how I see Célia.

"Inch alleluia under the nails
And if you want me
Touch me,
to confuse each other!
Hello m'alikoum, little sister!
I cry for you."

23. It's all "Hockey" Against Trisomy 21

Mathurin has a great idea: with his field hockey club in Lille, he regularly takes part in tournaments in aid of cystic fibrosis. And then he thought: "Why not for Down's syndrome?" That's kind of what I wanted to do with the Telethon. So, with all his friends, my brother decided to organize a meeting in Sainte-Catherine-lès-Arras in early January 2012. All the money raised will go to Down Up.

Mat is like my father, he wants to do everything. He's a coach, a referee, a team manager in his club's National 4 league, a member of the club's executive committee and treasurer of the regional roller field hockey committee.

Mat obtains permission for the venue. A large covered hall. It was thanks to him that it had been created by the town hall, when he was in 4th grade. He got hundreds of people to sign a petition for an indoor skatepark. He and his roller-skating buddies used to drop off petitions in all the sports stores. Back then, he did a lot of roller-blading and demonstrations. He was even sponsored by Intersport. He had seen the chief of staff of the mayor of Arras, Frédéric Leturque, and had been given his hall. Then he went to Australia.

I came with all my friends to support my brother and the Lille team. Amandine, Mario, Fleur… Most of them are here. All bundled up, because it's freezing. Even Amandine, who always confuses summer and winter, has her big red anorak with a scarf. She keeps it on even when she eats pasta.

To warm up, we shout: "Allez Mathurin!", "Allez Mat!" At the end, I even shout "Allez Lille!" So much for the Arras team. We follow the scores on the big electronic scoreboard. Lille wins.

Down Up made pasta carbonara and bolognese and rented a beer pump. My parents take care of the refreshment stand. I watch all the games. But especially my brother, with his helmet… It's impressive. And then there's his friend Xavier. He's the one who helped Mathurin when he fell off his skateboard and had a burst cheek. He'd had eight stitches in his face after jumping off a seven-step block. I didn't like that, but Mat keeps jumping all over the place.

My brother is all sweaty when he takes off his helmet, elbow pads, knee pads… but he's won: the day raises over a thousand euros for the association and I'm proud of my big brother.

24. Guest of the Week

Now, with my role as spokesperson for the collective, March will always be a busy month. March 21 is World Down Syndrome Day. We chose this date because it's the third month, like the third extra chromosome I have on pair 21. As the journalists get ready a few days before, I have to plan a few absences from work to make up for them...

Even when I'm away for a few hours, I have to recuperate. I finish later, for example. Sometimes I also take time off. It's the same when I go for check-ups, for my heart, for lab tests, for thyroid treatment, for scans... Every time they think I might have a new problem, a thrombosis, a pulmonary embolism or something else, they send me for new tests. The other day, I had stress tests on a treadmill. Ten minutes of brisk walking:

I almost collapsed. And always these blood tests… Five vials last time. A real horse's blood sample!

On March 16, I'm speaking with my father at the CESE (Conseil économique, social et environnemental), at the Palais d'Iéna. Now I'm used to speaking in public. Les Amis d'Éléonore is a collective of some thirty associations and three thousand people. Jean-Paul Delevoye is the President of the EESC. He's also the symposium's patron. He asked me to preside with him. There are a lot of people, it's impressive.

Robin blows on dandelions. Just inside the entrance, in the great hall, among eighty other photos from the book *Supplément d'âme*. You can also see me in front of the Assemblée nationale, and Stéph' at her home. We're all on large panels. These are the same photos we put up at the Islet Bon Secours for the Open House, and at the Belfry for the presentation of the medal to Manu.

My father wants more people with Down's syndrome to speak out and be heard. At the CESE, he talks about staying in a mainstream environment. And he's right. I explain that "I have friends in a closed environment and it's not good for them!" They're supermal in their own skin. I wouldn't want to be in their shoes. Then I talk about research needs.

A few days later, the website handicap.fr published an article about the day. It talks about me: "She was present that day, sitting at the podium with staggering aplomb, questioning everyone and moving the assembly to tears. The sincerity of her speech, her bursts of laughter and her little sobs are worth all the speeches alone." Yes, it's true, I don't always control all my emotions... The article also quotes the mother of a child with several disabilities who's fed up with working during the day, not sleeping at night, having to be a superhero all year round because there's no support. He also quotes my father: "It's not Eleonore who's handicapped, but society which has created a handicapping environment"; "The essential thing is not respect for the norm, but the culture of happiness." I always back up what my father says. He's my superhero.

On March 17 and 18, the TF1 team returns to see me for *C'est quoi l'amour? What happened to them?* I can tell her: "Welcome to my apartment! She had seen it under construction, now she sees it finished. Laurence, my helper, agrees to be filmed. We make a jam tart. It's a super-simple recipe. At school, Mrs. Bisbrouck and I always followed recipes. But she had to explain everything to us, because if she just said: "Add the whole eggs", some people forgot to break them and put them whole, straight into the flour. That's why you have to be square. At work, I'm always square and meticulous.

Laurence explains to TF1 that I'm "tidy" and that I'm gradually getting rid of my phobias: "Doing the dishes, having dirty hands, that's something she had a lot of trouble with, but now she's doing it." It's true, I hate it, that's why I didn't really enjoy my internship at the nursing home, it's not because of the old people. Laurence says that I'm "very independent" and that I'm becoming "more and more so".

The journalist also wants to know what my parents think about my new autonomy. So we go back to rue de Douai. On the sofa, my mother talks to me, in front of the camera, more about her own autonomy: "In the morning, hearing you laugh, your good mood... All that is something we still miss, yes." The journalist asks me:

"Do you miss your parents?

- A little less."

The team then films us at Leclerc. I go shopping with my parents, each of us going our own way. I just call my dad when I'm having a hard time with the shopping scan. TF1 also follows me to the Chapitre bookshop in Arras, rue Gambetta. Robin and I sign the book *Supplément d'âme*. Robin is still talking about how other people's looks hurt him. I tell him not to listen to people. To the camera, he says: "Yes, I listen to my girlfriend's advice, but I can't ignore it." I say, "I don't give a damn about what people think!"

The report ends at my place. I made my parents salmon. My father says he wants to see my future without him and my mother, that if tomorrow they disappeared... I don't like it when he talks like that.

I tell them that the next step for me "will be a civil union with my boyfriend, so I can have a big party. I've got to set a date."

Two days later, I'm off to Paris for the taping of *Le Magazine de la santé*. March 20, 2012, the eve of World Down Syndrome Day. I go with my mother to the Productions du 17 juin - Atlantis studio. My father can't come with us, he's working. I'm Michel Cymes and Marina Carrère d'Encausse's "guest of the day". Just before, my mother prepares me: "It's going to be okay, relax, take a good look at your interviewer." It's always the same words, but it puts me at ease. Marina also tells me that everything's going to be fine.

Marina: "Tomorrow is World Down's Syndrome Day. Its aim is to change and demystify the way people look at this disease. Éléonore, 26 years old, will be with us to talk about this view, which has often hurt her, but also about herself, her work and her life." I'm already settled in my armchair next to a shelf with huge jars of capsules that look like candy. I'm not really stressed, and it's like being in a living room. It's very colorful, just like at home, with pink and blue... Marina introduces Down's Syndrome Day and the "Trisomique, et alors?" campaign launched by a group of parents and associations. "And to mark the occasion, we'll be welcoming Éléonore Laloux..." It's my turn!

"Hello Eleonore.

- Hello Marina.

- You're 26 years old and have been working in a clinic for six years. What kind of work do you do in this clinic?

- I do alphabetical filing, addressing and enveloping. I make photocopies and send faxes."

Michel Cymes: "And how are things going today with your colleagues?

- At first, it was hard. Because I was talking to the walls. Little by little, people's opinions changed..."

Marina Carrère d'Encausse: "So things are going well today. Another thing that has changed in your life is that you now live in your own apartment. Were you the one who wanted to leave your parents? What made you leave?

- In fact, I wanted to follow in my brother's footsteps and get my parents off my back.

- Yes, that's right... I think your mom, who's not far away, will appreciate it... And then we found an apartment in a rather special residence... How's it going, what's it like?

- Basically... before it was the Islet Bon Secours, it was a clinic. That's where I started my training. Then my father and the architects created the îlot Bon Secours. In all, there are seventy-five apartments.

Michel Cymes: "And you have help in these apartments. You are totally autonomous... People come to help you?

- I'm self-sufficient and there are housekeepers who come four times a day."

I've made a big mistake! I don't know why I said "four times a day". They come four times a week for an hour, and that's more than enough. They're useful because there are things I don't know how to do: cleaning the windows, which are much too high for me, or opening a tin can because I'm afraid of cutting myself. The rest I can do on my own.

Marina Carrère d'Encausse: "And who helps you with what?

- Preparing my clothes according to the weather outside, for meals and also for housework.

- And what do you do at the weekend, like everyone else? Do you see friends?

- On weekends... I have lots of activities. I go to gym class with my mom, I take guitar lessons, I've been playing electric guitar forever. I go to appointments like speech therapy, physiotherapy, etc."

Michel Cymes: "When you have Down's Syndrome, you know that you're a little different from the others... You're proving today that you can have a very rich and happy life, but the way others look at you is sometimes a little insistent, not very pleasant. Today, when you walk down the street, when you go out, do you feel that people look at you a little strangely or not at all?

- Since the Friends of Éléonore collective was set up with my parents, attitudes are starting to change, and that's positive."

Marina Carrère d'Encausse: "So this group, Les Amis d'Éléonore, has produced a book called *Supplément d'âme*, featuring portraits of several people with Down's syndrome. It's very pretty and extremely interesting to read [...]. One last question, I'm going to be a little indiscreet, do you have a lover?

- Yes, I do. I have a boyfriend and we've been together for a year."

Michel Cymes: "His name is Benjamin... I snitch! And he works in the same clinic as you.

- Yes, he is. But he's not in the same department. He's in the pharmacy department. He does handling. In fact, he distributes medicines to all the departments."

Marina Carrère d'Encausse: "Éléonore, if you take stock of your life today, are you happy?

- Yes, I'm happy because I have the love of my parents, my whole family, my work colleagues, my boyfriend too..."

Michel Cymes: "All the happiness! Everything everyone wants. Thank you Éléonore."

Benjamin's father isn't going to be happy about us dropping his son's name. This is the last time I'll be talking about him in an interview. Benjamin and I had

to break up because of his father. It was too complicated. I cried a lot. But I still see him every day, every
lunchtime, in the canteen at work.

My colleagues tell me I'm making myself unhappy,
that I shouldn't see him so much. I think Benjamin will
always be alone because his father wants him to be
unhappy like him. But sometimes Benjamin reacts. He's
gone to the gendarmerie to lodge a complaint against
his father. I'd like to help him.

Every year since 2001, I've met up with the *Histoires
et Rêves d'Artois* troupe in the first week of September.
It's a sound and light show on the outskirts of Arras,
telling the story of the region. Three weekends, between
rehearsals and shows. I always arrive with a note for
Isabelle, my team leader. I thank her and tell her how
happy I am to be here. This show takes us through all
the eras, from prehistoric times onwards.

I love wearing my pretty pink dress and my big Belle
Époque hat, or parading close to the audience in a cart
pulled by draft horses, dressed as a peasant girl. Isabelle
just avoids giving me anything too dangerous to do:
holding a torch for the fire scene, running with heavy
rakes for the Napoleon III scene. I can't play the monks'
passage either: you have to position yourself in the dark
at a precise spot. It's bad enough I have to take off my
glasses because they're a bit too modern, but in the
dark... I even missed a scene once. With my beautiful

pink dress, I fell into the mud. I didn't have time to change for the next scene. What a disaster! So I always try to get a head start. I know I'm a bit slower, but I want to do everything perfectly, every year.

Three years ago, at the Parc d'Immercourt in Saint-Laurent-Blangy, I ended up in the emergency room. I'd twisted my foot in a rut getting off the cart.

In October, I shoot the second advertising campaign for Apreva, the mutual insurance company. "When health is good, everything is good!" That was their first slogan. My father coached me to say my new line. I rehearse with him two or three times to get it right, articulating it well: "… They talk to me straight, and I like that. For me, a health expert is just that…" I don't know why I chose these old glasses. Last time, they shot the spot at my place. My hair was a mess. I felt like it. It's weird, afterwards, to bump into each other in the street, like at Arras station the other day. Sometimes I even sit down next to myself to wait for the bus. I also see large signs of my head in the Minelle garden, and a few people recognize me. In the street, people recognize me because they've seen me on TV.

My mother has just had meniscus surgery. It's November 8, 2012, it's the Gossip concert and she doesn't want to miss it. I'm going anyway. In the evening, the nurse allows my mother to go, but she would have gone anyway. One of her legs is in a splint, and she drags herself around on crutches. She can't even bend her leg. The Red Cross helps my mother get to the disabled area and sit down with a chair in front of her to extend her leg. We're in a good position, and I've got plenty of room to dance. The band performs their new album, *A Joyful Noise,* and their earlier *Music For Men.* It's great! I love the songs *Perfect World, Into The Wild* and of course *Heavy Cross.*

Beth Ditto is on fire. She's smiling, rocking like I like. She rocks, she lets off steam and runs all over the stage. She's beautiful. I dance, I sing, I have a blast. At the end of the concert, Beth Ditto puts on a T-shirt with a picture of Barack Obama and introduces us to one of her French friends. That's it, I've seen her for real, and frankly, I'm not disappointed!

On December 2, I appear on TF1's *Sept à huit* presented by Harry Roselmack. I'm followed everywhere, from my parents' house, when I say goodbye to "my poisoned present", to my home, with my father inspecting the expired products in my fridge, or when I watch my *Zorro* series. And then we see Thibaut off to the bakery, Amandine making her star on the way to her job at the Soleil residence, Robin finding an internship in a theater and talking about Molière. And then there's me going crazy on Gossip in my room after work. Great report!

On the 6th, at the Palais Rameau in Lille, I was elected Géant 2012 in the "civil society" category, a prize awarded by the newspaper *La Voix du Nord* to honor the Nordistes of the year. There were two of us from Arrage in the running for the Géants trophy, along with Jules Laude, the mayor of Bullecourt. The newspaper is devoting two portraits to me this month. And I'm on the regional channel Wéo. I invite my parents over for a drink to celebrate my prize.

25. Well, Love You, too

I see Robin more and more often. We parted ways, but we've found each other again. Robin and I have known each other since we were toddlers. "*Mi chu d'ici, chu un gars de ch'Nord*" ("I'm from here, I'm a guy from the North"), that's how Robin says it. He likes to speak Ch'ti. He pulls out things he writes with his mother: "*Chu né à l'hôpital ed Beuvry. Ché sur, chu pas né din ché corons. Pourtant, min grand père yétot porion al fosse. Chef porion s'il vous plaît, Yallot travailler à l fosse avec sin casque et s'lampe, chétot dur mais yémot cha!*" ("I'm from here, I was born in Beuvry hospital. Of course, I wasn't born in the corons. But my grandfather was a foreman at the mine. Chief foreman, please. He went to work wearing his helmet and carrying a lamp. It was hard work, but he loved it!") When I said to him the other night at my place, "I love it when you talk like that!" He replied, *"Ben mi, j'chte ker mi auchi"* ("Well, I love you too") and kissed me on the neck.

Now he's starting to detach himself from his mother. He says he needs to "push the envelope". He told her he had "a private life" and "a girlfriend": me! That made me happy. I'd love it if he could cut ties with his mother and live with me. We have parties and intimate things that I can't really talk about, but it's complicated at the moment for him to settle down with me.

He told me he wanted to behave like a man. He also wants to stop acting altogether and devote himself to me. I don't think that's a good idea. His mother agrees with me. But he's already stopped. He writes poetry too. He does a lot of things, but he changes activities all the time. He wants to play the violin like his sister, he's learning sign language like his brother and English too. He wanted to be a singer after the film *Les Choristes*. I don't think he really knows what he wants.

He's also learning a little Spanish. Perhaps because of his family of travelers. His two older brothers spent two years on a Breton sailing boat when they were children. They went to the Caribbean. Then they lived in Canada and New Zealand. As for his sister, she settled in Venezuela... The other evening, I had an aperitif at home. I texted Stephanie too. I bought some sausage and cherry tomatoes, then a ham, olive and pistachio cake. Stephanie brought chocolates and Robin arrived a little later with a DVD of *Tinkerbell*. He was wearing his beautiful khaki and red T-shirt. He's got lots of cool T-shirts. As soon as he got home, he said he wanted to watch the film with me alone. I explained to him that it wasn't really fair to Stephanie. So we got to talking. He wanted to kiss me and kept saying words of love. I call him "Chéri".

Sometimes Robin gives me a flower. He also gave me a necklace with three hearts: love, joy and peace. Robin wants to start over with me. He likes to watch movies and TV shows together on the couch, like *L'Instit* or *Famille d'accueil*. We often watch TV and make out. Stéph' and I also cuddle, but they're friendly cuddles, like kisses all over the place, on the mouth... But we don't go too far. With Robin, it's all about love. He likes to kiss me on the stomach with his mouth. We go crazy together.

With him, I feel free with my body. I can show myself naked, I don't hide my scar. Not with my parents either, but my parents can only see the top or the bottom, because of my bra. Robin, I tell him he can touch it if he wants. He loves me just the way I am. Stephanie, I don't dare show him.

Last time, I cooked a recipe for salmon pasta that Robin had given me. Frankly, it was a real treat! He knows how to make *fajitas*. I like his relaxed, cool, friendly style. And his eyes and his mouth. He tells me I'm "beautiful, flirtatious, kind, easy to understand". He knows me well.

25. Well, Love You, too

Robin confides in me that he'd like to have a girlfriend like Celia. I thought that since I'm friends with Celia, he could be too, so the three of us could be together. That's what I'm looking for, a boyfriend or girlfriend who really loves me and has a stable job. I'm looking for love, work and someone who knows how to wash dishes properly. A gentleman or a *superwoman*! Robin, on the other hand, likes to do the ironing.

He accompanies me to the gym and we continue to watch *Famille d'accueil* on France 3. Robin would like me to move out and live with him. I'd like that too, but I don't want to screw up my apartment. It doesn't make sense to have two houses. He talks about children too. My father says that's nonsense, because it's a big responsibility. You have to get up at night, change him… I agree with my father. I'd like to be a mom, but I can't be pregnant. It's not good for my heart. Then we can adopt. I'd like that.

I've been on the pill since I got pimples and to avoid having children. But I don't really want to have sex, it hurts me. Robin and I do things differently.

26. *Le Grand Journal*

My brother is 31 now and lives with Anne-Claire. She's nice, a little Breton, a little Vietnamese. She often eats with baguettes at home. She spends weekends with Mat at my parents.' My brother and I were featured in *Fémina*, a women's magazine, for an article on siblings. Mathurin talks about our complicity. He says he's sorry he wasn't there when people made fun of me at school. He talks about the text messages I send to "my beloved brother". Sometimes I give him a hug and say, "I love you." And I kiss him. He replies, "My sister's great," and that he loves me too. I want my brother to be happy. Like I do with Robin.

In any case, Mat got the year off to a bad start. He's smashed his face in again. This time on a snowboard. "Glenoid bulge out of place, biceps tendon rupture". Glenoid? My big Robert Collège doesn't know that one. Mat sees three surgeons in a row. They don't know what to do with him. So they operate anyway. Thanks to his little camera, his GoPro, Mat was able to film his entire fall, which you can now watch on Vimeo. In the footage, you can see him jumping all over the place, and it looks like he's having a good laugh at falling, just like when he was given shots as a child.

On March 21, 2013, I'm on rue des Cévennes, in the 15th arrondissement of Paris. I'm waiting in a dressing room with two sofas, a coffee table with drinks, sweets, flowers and a small flat screen showing the show live. Next door, there are dressing rooms for Nikos, *The Voice* contestants, Jean-Michel Apathie and Valérie Trierweiler. It's with her that I'll be appearing on Canal Plus's *Grand Journal.* She's the godmother of the tenth World Down's Syndrome Day.

You can follow the recording everywhere, even from the make-up rooms. Everyone comes to say hello to me and my parents, to chat, ask questions and explain how things are going to work. Michel Denisot is interested in me because he has a family member with Down's Syndrome who works in an ESAT. Augustin kisses me. He looks at the book *Supplément d'âme.* He says it's a beautiful book and that he'll talk about it on the show. Daphné Bürki also kisses me and rolls up her sleeves to show me her tattoos.

As we stand in the hall watching the big TV set, Nikos comes over to say hello. Nikos is the Greek guy who hosts *The Voice*. He's a good-looking guy, but I prefer Karine Ferri. I say to him, "Ah, Nikos, you're presenting *The Voice right now*, but I'm watching and I know the other presenter, Karine Ferri, who presents *The Voice. More.*

- Ah yes! Do you like Karine?

- A lot."

I like her, and she was the girlfriend of Gregory Lemarchal, who died. So Nikos asks me if I'd like to meet her. He takes me by the hand and leads me straight into the dressing room with the *The Voice* contestants. I ask Karine Ferri: "Are you Gregory Lemarchal's wife?" She replies, "Yes". I stayed about fifteen minutes in the dressing room and chatted with the candidates.

My mother warns me to be careful when it starts, that I'm going to be filmed a lot. I have to be careful not to show off too much, or open my mouth, or stare all over the place, as sometimes happens when I'm a bit stressed. In the make-up room, I had my hair done up like a firecracker. Valérie Trierweiler came to chat with me. She's beautiful and wears high heels. I don't know how she walks.

Michel Denisot begins: "A special program to mark World Down's Syndrome Day and, as promised, two guests, one who lives with Down's Syndrome on a daily basis, the other who has made it a battle, here are Éléonore Laloux and Valérie Trierweiler." We both arrive on the set of Le *Grand Journal*. Valérie Trierweiler has stage fright, more than me, and with her heels, she's especially afraid of falling down the stairs, so I hold her hand. When the big door opens, I'm impressed. The stage is huge and everyone applauds. Michel Denisot comes to shake our hands. Then we all sit down on the seats and Valérie Trierweiler talks about her commitment, her little neighbor Françoise, who used to come to her house when she was little and who had Down's syndrome, then the young boys with Down's syndrome she welcomed into the Élysée kitchens...

Michel Denisot (MD): "How's your life going, Eleonore, are you working?

- Yes, I work at a private hospital in Arras. I get on well with my colleagues. They're nice to me."

People always ask me the same questions, so I always give the same answers. I've been working at Les Bonnettes for eight years now. Stephanie will sign her first permanent contract on February 1, 2014.

MD : "How's your day-to-day life?

- I have a helper who comes once a week to help me maintain my apartment, for my clothes and also for the meal and...

- Are you self-sufficient?

- ... And I'm independent."

Daphné Bürki (DB): "And at work, it's the same thing? What do you do at work?

- I do addressing, enveloping, alphabetical filing. I send faxes and make photocopies."

MD: "Do you have a fiancé?"

DB: "Intrusive question…

- I have one, and it's in my residence too.

- Éléonore, it's something you experience every day, the way others look at you. How do you feel about it?

- I'm just like everyone else. I live like everyone else. And with the collective, attitudes are changing. I can really feel it."

MD : "What do you do when the looks are… not right?

- I ignore them, directly!"

Valérie Trierweiler: "I need to learn this." On the set, parents of children with Down's syndrome also testify, like Isabelle and Augustin, and then Jacqueline London, president of AFRT (Association française pour la recherche sur la trisomie 21[14]). During the commercials, I chat with Daphné Bürki and Augustin Trapenard.

At the end of the show, the technicians come to congratulate me. Then we chat with Valérie Trierweiler and Michel Denisot. Jean-Michel Aphatie greets me. He seems a little cold to Michel Denisot, but he's fine with me. My mother meets up with a friend who works at Canal: Nicolas Nerrant. He's a Blur fan. He used to write

____

14. French Association for Research on Trisomy 21.

for their fanzine, but she hadn't seen him for ten years. Since a concert... She was very happy.

The day after the *Grand Journal*, I'm invited to speak on United Nations radio. I talk about my job, Canal Plus, Down's syndrome... But the journalist calls me a bit "gaga". When she asks me what message I want to send, I talk about doctors: "I'd like to change the way people look at things and send a message to doctors, that they should stop saying everything that's negative, that they should stop talking about 'chromosomal aberration', because it's not true. We're not poisons, we're not like monsters, we live like other people." Then I tell her I'll go to New York if I'm invited.

In May, we celebrate the birthdays of my grandfather Padé and Grandma's brother Émile. They are both 90 years old. As there's no more room in Moyenneville for the growing family, we gather at a restaurant, Domaine des Cascades, in Wancourt. I go there with Robin, who's a bit lost in the middle of my family. So I keep an eye on him and tell him to stay close to me. There were a hundred and twenty of us! Robin thought I had a lot of cousins and a "very cumbersome" family. He wanted to give a book he'd made with a hedgehog for Padé, but he missed the hedgehog: it had no nose and no eyes. For his 90th birthday, Padé got a GPS to stick in his white Corsa, an iPad with a stylus and a computer. Now, with the computer, Padé plays solitaire and Grandma searches for recipes on www.marmiton.org

In the summer of 2013, I spend my vacations at my uncle Pascal's, my mother's brother. He has a Harley Davidson Road King Classic. Superb! He had come to show it to me on my 26th birthday in Arras. It was a surprise. He'd just bought it. He does a lot of *biker* rallies, in Rome, Barcelona... With his Harley, we set off for Narbonne-Plage. Forty kilometers. I hold on to the waistband of his pants. We cross all the small roads in the garrigue, the Clape massif, the olive groves. No time to listen to the cicadas. Sometimes, on the Harley, he yells at me, "ÇA VA?" Then I answer him the same way, shouting so that he hears, "OUI, ÇA VA!" And then I say, "Go for it, think of your beer waiting for you!" So he goes for it.

In mid-July, I'm again at the Splendid in Lille for Devendra Banhart, as in 2007. I'm stunned every time I see him. I love the way he moves. And then he does weird things with his voice, with his mouth, and he rolls his r's. I think it's because he's such a great singer. I think it's because he grew up in Venezuela. He's super funny when he sings: *I Feel Just Like a Child*. The one he sang at *Taratata*. As always, I leave my parents behind and slide right in front. I'm small, I don't take up much room, everyone lets me pass: "Pardon, pardon... Pardon..."

At the end of the concert, the drummer crosses the stage and hands me his drumsticks. He usually throws them away, but now he's just giving them to me. I was thrilled. My mother knows the Splendid well, so at the end of the concert, we joined Devendra with a dozen other people, next to their bus. She asks him a few questions about the band Suede, which he quotes in his song. He says it's because he's a fan. And so are we! We saw them in 2002, at La Route du Rock in Saint-Malo. He dedicates the inside double page of his latest album *Mala* to us with our initials: EL and ML for Éléonore and Maryse Laloux, then draws a pitcher, lips and his initials...At the end of November, my parents learn that I have a constriction in my heart. They were worried.

"I've been eating dry food ever since,

I have bits of skeleton that do anything,

Pieces of me that just don't care."

It's Soan, from *Séquelles*. I love that song, as well as *À tire-d'aile* and *Conquistador*. A little concert is good for everyone. Soan is playing in Lille on December 1st, at La Péniche, on the Deûle. So let's go. I've already seen him live, but I just love his scruffy, rock punk style, his gravelly voice, his music, his lyrics... I've got all three of his albums.

When we arrive, the room is packed. I squeeze in at the front, as usual. I'll meet my parents at the end of the concert. Soan sings some thirty songs, for over two hours. Halfway through the concert, he holds out his hand and takes me on stage. I don't understand what's happening to me. The audience applauds. I close my eyes and rest my head against him. He kisses me. I was so happy. A few days later, I received a photo on Facebook of Soan and me. It was taken by someone in the audience. I'll put it by my bed.

When I show the photo, I tell everyone that I did a duet with Soan, but my mother says that's not what a "duet" is. You have to sing. Still, it was a beautiful duet…

27. Break Everything!

I can't move and I have to keep this mask on my face. I'm stressed and crying. They prepare me for a catheterization and coronary angiography, under anesthesia, at groin level. Monday, February 3, 2014, I'm in hospital, at the CHRU de Lille, cardiology department. I don't want it to happen again like when I was little.

We don't really know what's wrong with me, so I'm going to have a lot of tests. Blood tests, electro-cardiograms... It's my heart that's still worrying me. I don't like hospitals. I don't want any more operations. The doctors don't even know if it's still possible, because I've been so open.

I think back to the day before, when we went out to eat with Mathurin and his girlfriend. Lamb mouse with honey and crème brûlée. It was delicious! I want to go home soon.

... Afterwards, in the evening, here, my mother shaved me all over, showered me with Betadine... She's there beside me. She's always there for me. We even lent her a cot for the night. Luckily I've got a TV in the bedroom so I can watch *Plus belle la vie* and my mother can have a few laughs.

In the afternoon, I see Dr. Godart. He explains everything to me: I've got a nice left coronary, a right coronary that's too tight to see anything, and a mitral valve that's not so good. I have to start treatment for heart failure this evening. I now have two medications to take: Levothyrox for my thyroid and Triatec for my heart, plus my vitamins. I'll also have to have another coroscan.

Later, I'll see a surgeon who'll tell me if I need surgery on my sternum. Dr. Godart tells me that it could be a bone that's causing me all this pain. It's like when my father drives his Lexus over the cobblestones of the Grand'Place or Place des Héros in Arras: my depressed sternum pushes inwards. That's why I'm often out of breath and in pain.

Doctor Godart looks pleased. He says to himself, "We're going to find out what the hell it is!" That's what I think. I'm glad my mother's here. I need her more and more, to wash me, to help me go to the bathroom, for meals, to open the window... It's really hot as hell in here! She pampers me. We watch *Famille d'accueil* on TV... The next day, Dr Godart tells me about an MRI this time. He explains that I'll be the one to decide whether or not to go ahead with the thoracic surgery, because it's very painful. "You have to break everything." That's what he said. Break everything... Frankly, it's scary!

Like yesterday and the day before, this Wednesday I'm having an electrocardiogram and blood pressure check. I'm still at 8.4. I'm also given a chest X-ray before I'm discharged. Manu picks me and my mother up at the hospital. His Lexus doesn't do me any favors, especially as we drive through the cobblestone squares of Arras on our way to Becquart's. I feel like I've been stabbed. I feel like I'm being stabbed in the left side and in the front, at sternum level. But we're going to buy crépinettes and I love them!

I'm staying with my parents. I'm going to be pampered again... I think the treatment for my heart is knocking me out. I want to sleep.

28. *"In a beautiful world"*

I keep on fighting. That's what I've been doing since I was born, as Mum says. I have serious health problems today, but I'm not poison. Not to my parents, anyway. They love me and so do I, and we're going to sort out these heart problems.

At the residence, we all took different paths. But we're making progress. Last week, Stephanie signed her first permanent contract at the Beaurains library. Robin is looking for work, but I know he'll find it soon. We've all been lucky to see people, different people, all the time, at school, at work... And that's why we're moving forward. If I'd been put in a closed environment, I'd have gone completely mad.

My father says he has nothing against specialized institutions, that they can exist too. But he says that people with Down's Syndrome should be supported in an ordinary environment, not prevented from being with everyone else. I'm against the closed environment. For me, it's like a psychiatric hospital!

I don't advise parents to put their children in there. It's too sad. But it's not their fault: they don't know. I have a lot of friends in a closed environment. I can see they don't feel good about themselves. I'd be miserable and depressed if I were in their shoes.

My father and I are going to get Gilles-Emmanuel out of his ESAT[15] because he's really fed up. He wants to leave. My father is talking to the manager of the McDonald's in Beaurains to see if he can take him on. I'd prefer us to support people with Down's syndrome in an open environment and then help research to put an end to this disease once and for all. I know it's possible. Soon. That's why I dream of a "Trisothon". I'd like it to be over soon.

Benjamin is more than a boyfriend, he's my ex-boyfriend. I don't want him to be unhappy anymore either. His father is violent and won't let him go. But Benjamin is over 18 and he's not alone. There's me, my father, his boss at the clinic where we both work, his psychologist. That's what I keep telling him. He's got to go, fast. Live on his own, without his father. Manu and I have to help Benjamin find an apartment.

---

15. Établissement et services d'aide par le travail.

Robin wants us to move, to really live together. He wants us to live in a small house, but not too small. I'm fine like this, each with his own apartment. Robin insists. He wants us to be together and have children. But children are a big responsibility. Kids plus my job are too much for me. My future now is with a boyfriend and no kids.

Seeing each other one night a week is fine with me. It's nice. Besides, I mustn't get carried away. I get palpitations when I'm happy.

Robin wants me to sleep with him all the time. I can't do that. I have to get up in the morning. Maybe later, when he's working too... He's always taking sign language lessons. I don't know why, he doesn't know any deaf or hard-of-hearing people. And I don't know enough sign language to talk to him. Like me, he needs to find a stable job where things don't move too fast.

I often want to sleep with him too, but all I have at home is a small bed and a sofa that clicks. I have to change the rules I proposed at the residence. Besides, rules shouldn't apply to lovers. Rules are for other people!

And then I want to see Robin happy, hear him sing Adele's *Someone Like You*, like he does when he's happy, and then Katy Perry's *Firework*, or his other old people music, and go off like fireworks, like in the video. I want to see him when I want to see him, and I want to go beyond volume 7 when I put on Radiohead's *Creep* to

28. "In a beautiful world"

listen to my music loud and clear. It makes me cry, it's so beautiful.

"... Your skin makes me cry
You float like a feather
In a beautiful world
I wish I was special
You're so fuckin' special..."

Robin, I'm telling you, I'm going to help you again. You'll see. We love each other. We'll be together. I'll cook for you. You'll do the laundry, the ironing, because I know you're a man. I want you to show the others: you're an adult. But you've got to move on, stop listening to other people, stop listening to your mother. As I said in the press conference video, you've just got an extra chromosome. We don't give a damn about other people's looks!

Table of Contents

Table of contents

Best sellers Max Milo Editions

Hitler's banker, Jean-François Bouchard

Confessions of a forger, Éric Piedoie Le Tiec

The Koran and the flesh, Ludovic-Mohamed Zahed

Governing by fake news, Jacques Baud

Governing by chaos, Collectif

A political history of food, Paul Ariès

Mad in U.S.A.: The ravages of the "American model",
Michel Desmurget

Mondial soccer club geopolitics, Kévin Veyssière

Putin: Game master?, Jacques Braud

Treatise on the three impostors: Moses, Jesus, Muhammad,
The Spirit of Spinoza

TV Lobotomy, Michel Desmurget